cooking from
the market *fruit*

cooking from the market *fruit*

MURDOCH BOOKS

contents

introduction

In a growing trend towards buying food that is fresh and in season, more of us are shopping locally from grower's markets. We want to reconnect with our food and the people who grow it. *Cooking from the Market* gives you tips on what to look for when buying your fruit and how to store and prepare it. And, most importantly, it features a selection of recipes that showcase each fruit to perfection.

citrus fruit

grapefruit

- The peak season for grapefruit is from winter to spring.
- When buying grapefruit, note that they are classified as white, pink or ruby, which refers to the colour of the flesh and not the skin.
- Choose fruit that feel heavy for their size, with tight skin and no soft spots.
- Store for 3 weeks in the crisper of the fridge, or about 1 week at room temperature.

Preparation

Like most citrus, the membranes and pith are bitter. To remove them, use a small knife to slice off all the peel and pith and cut between the membranes to remove the segments. Or simply cut the fruit in half, sprinkle with sugar and flash under the grill (broiler), then scoop out the flesh with a spoon or a special grapefruit knife.

The grapefruit is the largest known citrus and is named for the fact that it grows in heavy grapelike clusters. A relatively modern fruit, the grapefruit was discovered in Barbados about 300 years ago and is thought to be a cross between a pomelo and sweet orange. Toss grapefruit segments through seafood or green salads, or mix with Campari to make a refreshing sorbet or granita.

Ginger and grapefruit pudding with mascarpone cream

SERVES 6

1 large ruby grapefruit
40 g (1½ oz/⅓ cup) drained stem ginger
   in syrup, plus 3 teaspoons syrup
1½ tablespoons golden syrup or honey
125 g (4½ oz) unsalted butter, softened
115 g (4 oz/½ cup) caster (superfine) sugar
2 eggs, at room temperature
185 g (6½ oz/1½ cups) self-raising flour
1 teaspoon ground ginger
4 tablespoons milk

mascarpone cream

125 g (4½ oz/heaped ½ cup) mascarpone
   cheese
125 ml (4 fl oz/½ cup) cream
1 tablespoon icing (confectioners') sugar,
   sifted

Preheat the oven to 170°C (325°F/Gas 3). Grease six 170 ml (5½ fl oz/⅔ cup) ramekins or pudding moulds (basins).

Finely grate 2 teaspoons of zest from the grapefruit and set aside. Cut the grapefruit widthways, about one-third of the way down, to give two uneven sized pieces. Peel the larger piece of grapefruit, removing any white pith, and cut the flesh into six 1 cm (½ inch) slices. Squeeze 3 teaspoons of juice from the remaining grapefruit half. Finely chop the stem ginger.

Combine the grapefruit juice, ginger syrup and golden syrup in a small bowl. Divide the mixture among the ramekins and top with a slice of grapefruit, trimming to fit.

Put the butter and sugar in a bowl and beat with electric beaters until pale and smooth. Beat in the eggs, one at a time. Sift in the flour and ground ginger, add the grapefruit zest, chopped ginger and milk and mix well. Divide the mixture among the ramekins.

Cover each ramekin with foil and put them in a deep roasting tin. Pour in enough boiling water to come halfway up the sides of the ramekins. Cover the roasting tin with foil, sealing the edges well. Bake the puddings for 30–35 minutes, or until set.

To make the mascarpone cream, mix the mascarpone cheese, cream and icing sugar in a small bowl until smooth. To serve, gently invert the puddings onto serving plates and serve with the mascarpone cream.

Warm lamb, watercress and citrus salad

SERVES 4

dressing
1 tablespoon red wine vinegar
1 garlic clove, crushed
$1/2$ teaspoon honey
2 teaspoons walnut oil
$1^1/2$ tablespoons olive oil

300 g ($10^1/2$ oz) lamb fillets
1 tablespoon olive oil
2 oranges
1 small pink grapefruit
200 g (7 oz) watercress sprigs
$1/2$ small red onion, thinly sliced

To make the dressing, put the vinegar, garlic, honey, walnut oil and olive oil in a small bowl, season with sea salt and freshly ground black pepper and whisk to combine.

Cut the lamb fillets in half and season with freshly ground black pepper. Heat the olive oil in a frying pan over high heat and cook the lamb for 3–4 minutes, turning until browned all over but still a little pink in the middle. Season with sea salt and remove the lamb from the heat, cover and set aside.

Using a small knife, peel the oranges and grapefruit, taking care to remove the bitter white pith. Working over a bowl to catch any juices, carefully remove the grapefruit and orange segments by cutting between the white membrane and the flesh. Put the citrus segments in the bowl with the juices.

Cut the lamb on the diagonal into 2.5 cm (1 inch) thick slices and add to the bowl, along with the watercress and red onion. Pour the dressing over the salad and lightly toss to coat.

Avocado and grapefruit salad

SERVES 4

2 ruby grapefruit
1 ripe avocado
200 g (7 oz) watercress sprigs
1 French shallot, thinly sliced
1 tablespoon sherry vinegar
3 tablespoons olive oil

Using a small knife, peel each grapefruit, taking care to remove the bitter white pith. Working over a bowl to catch any juices for the dressing, carefully remove the grapefruit segments by cutting between the white membrane and the flesh. Squeeze out any juice remaining in the membranes into the bowl. Put the grapefruit segments into another bowl.

Peel the avocado, cut it in half and remove the stone. Cut the flesh into 2 cm ($3/4$ inch) wedges and place in the bowl with the grapefruit segments. Add the watercress and shallot.

Put 1 tablespoon of the reserved grapefruit juice in a small bowl with the vinegar, olive oil and a little sea salt and freshly ground black pepper. Whisk together well, then pour the dressing over the salad and toss to coat.

Divide the salad among serving plates and serve immediately.

kumquat

Although it resembles a small orange, the kumquat (or cumquat) is technically not a citrus at all. It has a genus, *Fortunella*, all its own, mainly because it can be eaten whole — pith, skin and seeds included — and because it has only three to six segments, unlike a true citrus, which has between eight and fifteen segments.

Varieties

Nagami The most commonly grown kumquat, this is slightly oval in shape, with tart flesh and quite pungent, sweet skin.

Marumi This variety is rounder in shape and is generally sweeter than the nagami.

Meiwa A pale-coloured, thick-skinned kumquat, this variety is often seedless and is the best type for eating raw.

Buying and storing

- The peak season for kumquats is from winter to mid-spring.
- Choose kumquats that have firm, shiny, unblemished skins. Check for any signs of mould or fruit that have been squashed.
- Store kumquats in the fridge for up to 2 weeks, or at cool room temperature for several days.

Preparation

Kumquats don't need to be peeled before use, and although they can be eaten raw, they are quite tart. For this reason, they are often preserved in a brandied syrup or simmered in a sugar syrup first and then used as a flavouring in ice creams, or in fruit compotes and other desserts. Kumquats can also be pickled and served with smoked or game meats or made into a marmalade.

Caramelised kumquats with honey parfait

SERVES 4

90 g (3¼ oz/¼ cup) honey
4 egg yolks, at room temperature
300 ml (10½ fl oz) cream, whipped
1 tablespoon orange liqueur, such as
    Grand Marnier
500 g (1 lb 2 oz) kumquats
350 g (12 oz/1½ cups) caster (superfine)
    sugar

Put the honey in a small saucepan and bring to the boil. Whisk the egg yolks in a bowl until thick and pale, then add the hot honey in a slow stream, whisking constantly. Allow to cool, then gently fold in the whipped cream and liqueur. Pour the mixture into six 125 ml (4 fl oz/½ cup) ramekins or pudding moulds (basins). Freeze for 4 hours, or until firm.

Wash the kumquats and prick the skins with a skewer. Put the kumquats in a large saucepan, cover with boiling water and simmer for 20 minutes. Strain the kumquats and reserve 500 ml (17 fl oz/2 cups) of the liquid. Return the liquid to the saucepan, add the sugar and stir over medium heat until the sugar has dissolved, then increase the heat and boil for 10 minutes. Add the kumquats and simmer for 20 minutes, or until the kumquats are soft and the skins are smooth and shiny. Remove the pan from the heat, leaving the kumquats in the pan, and set aside to cool. Lift the kumquats out of the syrup, reserving the syrup.

To serve, dip the ramekins in hot water for 5–10 seconds, then invert the parfait onto serving plates. Serve with the caramelised kumquats on the side and some syrup spooned over the top.

note Kumquats in syrup also make a delicious topping for ice cream, sponge cakes and puddings.

Kumquats are native to China and have long been cultivated there and in other Asian countries such as Japan and Vietnam. The tree is a symbol of prosperity and is often given as a gift during Chinese New Year. The English translation of the Chinese *gam gwat* is 'golden orange'.

lemon

Although rarely eaten on its own, the lemon is a true kitchen staple, lending a delightful sharp but sweet flavour and fresh fragrance to myriad dishes. Its juice and grated zest are used in dressings and drinks, in sweet and savoury sauces, and in a plethora of cakes and desserts. Lemons were even used in early times in witchcraft, in antidotes for various poisons and as antiseptics. We squeeze a lemon into a glass of hot water and honey as a remedy for a cold, lemon juice is used in skin preparations to clear up oily complexions and as a non-chemical bleach for hair. And how would life be if we didn't have a thin slice of lemon to finish a cup of perfectly brewed black tea?

Varieties

Different varieties of lemons have different degrees of acidity, so consider this when buying them. Lisbon and eureka lemons are the most common varieties, and these have vivid yellow skin and acidic, juicy flesh. Use in any recipe that requires lemon juice or zest. Myer lemons are sweeter, have thin orangey yellow skin, a full flavour and high yield of juice. Use in drinks such as homemade lemonade, and in desserts.

Buying and storing

- Lemons are available year-round.

- Buy lemons with firm, glossy skin and those that are heavy for their size. Avoid any that are tinged with green, as these aren't fully developed and won't have the best flavour.

- Check the lemons in your fruit bowl often — if one starts to grow mouldy, the mould will soon spread to the other lemons nearby.

- Store lemons in the fridge for up to 2 weeks, or for 1 week at cool room temperature.

Preparation

Most shop-bought lemons are sold coated with a thin layer of wax, which prevents them from drying out. Buy unwaxed ones from your local market; otherwise, scrub them lightly with warm water before use (don't scrub too hard, as the zest contains the aromatic citrus oils).

To use the zest of a lemon, grate it finely, turning the fruit as you go so you don't grate any of the bitter white pith. For thin strips of lemon zest, use a small knife to remove the peel (the zest) in slices. Lay the slices, pith side up, on a board and use the knife to scrape off any remaining pith, then cut into strips or shreds. These can be blanched in boiling water before use, to remove some of the volatile flavours.

Not only are **lemons** high in vitamin C but they also contain flavonoids, an antioxidant thought to help ward off cancer and heart disease. The membranes between the lemon segments are a good source of pectin, a fibre that can be helpful in controlling blood cholesterol.

Orange and lemon syrup cake

SERVES 10–12

3 lemons
3 oranges
250 g (9 oz) cold unsalted butter, chopped
700 g (1 lb 9 oz/3 cups) caster (superfine) sugar
6 eggs, lightly beaten
375 ml (13 fl oz/1 1/2 cups) milk
375 g (13 oz/3 cups) self-raising flour, sifted

Preheat the oven to 160°C (315°F/Gas 2–3). Grease a 24 cm (9 1/2 inch) spring-form cake tin and line the base and side with baking paper.

Finely grate the zest from the lemons and oranges to give 3 tablespoons each of lemon and orange zest, then squeeze the fruit to give 185 ml (6 fl oz/3/4 cup) lemon juice and 185 ml (6 fl oz/3/4 cup) orange juice.

Put the butter, 460 g (1 lb/2 cups) of the sugar and 1 tablespoon each of the lemon and orange zest in a saucepan over low heat. Stir until the butter has melted and the sugar has dissolved, then pour into a bowl.

Add half the beaten egg, half the milk and half the flour, beating with electric beaters until just combined. Add the remaining egg, milk and flour and beat until just smooth — do not overmix.

Pour the batter into the prepared cake tin and bake for 1 1/4 hours, or until a skewer inserted into the centre of the cake comes out clean — cover the cake with foil if it browns too quickly. Remove the cake from the oven and allow to cool in the tin.

Put the fruit juice in a saucepan with the remaining citrus zest, remaining sugar and 125 ml (4 fl oz/1/2 cup) water. Stir over low heat until the sugar has dissolved, then increase the heat and boil for 10 minutes, or until the mixture thickens slightly.

Pour the hot syrup over the cooled cake. Leave in the tin for a further 10 minutes, then invert onto a serving plate.

The orange and lemon syrup cake will keep for up to 4 days, stored in a cool place in an airtight container.

Lemon delicious

SERVES 4–6

60 g (2 1/4 oz) unsalted butter, at room
   temperature
185 g (6 1/2 oz/3/4 cup) sugar
2 teaspoons finely grated lemon zest
3 eggs, separated
30 g (1 oz/1/4 cup) self-raising flour
185 ml (6 fl oz/3/4 cup) milk
4 tablespoons lemon juice
icing (confectioners') sugar, to dust
thick (double/heavy) cream, to serve

Preheat the oven to 180°C (350°F/Gas 4).
Grease a 1.25 litre (44 fl oz/5 cup) ovenproof
ceramic dish.

Using an electric beater, beat the butter,
sugar and lemon zest together in a bowl
until the mixture is pale and fluffy. Gradually
add the egg yolks, beating well after each
addition, then fold in the flour and milk
alternately to make a smooth, thin batter.
Stir in the lemon juice; don't worry if the
batter looks separated.

Whisk the egg whites in a clean, dry bowl
until firm peaks form, then, with a large metal
spoon, fold a third of the egg white into the
batter to loosen. Gently fold in the remaining
egg white, being careful not to overmix.

Pour the batter into the prepared dish and
place in a large roasting tin. Pour enough
hot water into the tin to come a third of
the way up the side of the dish. Bake for
55 minutes, or until the pudding has risen
and the top is golden and firm to touch.
Leave for 5 minutes before serving. Dust
with icing sugar and serve with cream.

Warm olives
with lemon and herbs

SERVES 6

350 g (12 oz/2 cups) black kalamata olives
4 tablespoons olive oil
1 teaspoon fennel seeds
2 garlic cloves, finely chopped
a pinch of cayenne pepper
finely grated zest and juice of 1 lemon
1 tablespoon finely chopped flat-leaf
   (Italian) parsley
1 tablespoon finely chopped
   coriander (cilantro)

Rinse the olives, drain and put them in a
saucepan with enough water to cover. Bring
to the boil and cook for 5 minutes, then drain
in a sieve.

Add the olive oil and fennel seeds to the
saucepan and heat until fragrant. Add the
drained olives, garlic, cayenne pepper, lemon
zest and juice. Toss for 2 minutes, or until the
olives are heated through.

Transfer to a bowl and toss with the parsley
and coriander. Serve hot as part of an
antipasti selection or with crusty bread to
soak up the juices.

Real lemon pie

SERVES 8

filling
4 thin-skinned lemons
460 g (1 lb/2 cups) caster (superfine) sugar
4 eggs, lightly beaten

310 g (11 oz/2½ cups) plain (all-purpose)
   flour
80 g (2¾ oz/⅓ cup) caster (superfine)
   sugar
225 g (8 oz) cold unsalted butter, chopped
2–3 tablespoons iced water
milk, for brushing
cream, to serve

Start making the filling a day ahead. Wash the lemons well, then dry. Peel two lemons, removing all the white pith with a small knife, then slice the flesh very thinly, removing any seeds. Leave the other two lemons unpeeled and slice very thinly, removing any seeds. Place in a bowl with the sugar and stir until the lemon slices are coated. Cover and leave to stand overnight.

Sift the flour and a pinch of salt into a large bowl, then stir in the sugar. Using your fingertips, lightly rub in the butter until the mixture resembles breadcrumbs. Make a well in the centre and gradually add most of the iced water, mixing with a flat-bladed knife until a rough dough forms, adding a little extra iced water if necessary.

Turn out onto a lightly floured work surface, then gently gather the dough together. Divide the dough in half and press into a round disc. Cover with plastic wrap and refrigerate for 30 minutes, or until firm.

Preheat the oven to 180°C (350°F/Gas 4). Lightly grease a 23 cm (9 inch) pie dish that is at least 3 cm (1¼ inches) deep.

Roll out one portion of dough into a 30 cm (12 inch) circle. Roll the sheet of dough around the rolling pin, then lift and ease it into the pie dish, gently pressing to fit the side. Roll out the second portion of dough, onto a bread board, large enough to fit the top of the pie. Cover the pastry with plastic wrap and return to the fridge for 20 minutes.

Meanwhile, finish preparing the filling. Measure out 750 ml (26 fl oz/3 cups) of the lemon slices and liquid. Place in a bowl with the beaten eggs, stirring to mix well.

Spoon the mixture into the chilled pastry shell, then cover with the remaining pastry circle, trimming the pastry and crimping the edges to seal. Reroll the pastry scraps and cut out decorative shapes. Place on top of the pie and brush with milk.

Bake for 50–55 minutes, or until the pastry is golden brown. Remove from the oven and allow to cool slightly. Serve straight from the dish, with cream for drizzling over.

variation To make an apple pie, peel, core and thinly slice 5 apples. Combine a pinch of cinnamon with 3 tablespoons caster (superfine) sugar and toss with the apples. Fill the pie, cover with the pastry lid and make some slashes in the top. Dust with caster sugar and bake for 50 minutes.

If you have a glut of **lemons**, juice them and freeze the juice in iceblock trays for up to 3 months (transfer the iceblocks to a sealed container in the freezer once frozen). Heat the lemons in a bowl of hot water or put them in the microwave for a few seconds before juicing, as this helps the juices run.

Lemon, herb and fish risotto

SERVES 4

1.25 litres (44 fl oz/5 cups) fish stock
60 g (2 1/4 oz) butter
400 g (14 oz) skinless firm white fish fillets,
    cut into 3 cm (1 1/4 inch) cubes
1 onion, finely chopped
1 garlic clove, crushed
a large pinch of saffron threads
330 g (11 3/4 oz/1 1/2 cups) risotto rice
2 tablespoons lemon juice
1 tablespoon chopped flat-leaf (Italian)
    parsley
1 tablespoon snipped chives
1 tablespoon chopped dill
lemon slices, to garnish
herb sprigs, to garnish

Pour the stock into a saucepan and bring to the boil. Reduce the heat, then cover and keep at simmering point.

Melt half the butter in a frying pan. Add the fish in batches and fry over medium–high heat for 3–4 minutes, or until the fish is just cooked through, turning once. Remove from the pan and set aside. Keep warm.

Melt the remaining butter in a large heavy-based saucepan. Add the onion and garlic to the pan and sauté over medium heat for 5 minutes, or until the onion has softened. Add the saffron and rice and stir to coat, then add 125 ml (4 fl oz/1/2 cup) of the simmering stock and cook, stirring constantly, over low heat until all the stock is absorbed. Continue adding the stock, 125 ml (4 fl oz/1/2 cup) at a time, stirring constantly, and waiting until the stock is absorbed before adding more. Cook for 20–25 minutes, or until the rice is tender and creamy; you may need slightly less or more stock.

Stir in the lemon juice, parsley, chives and dill. Add the fish and stir gently. Spoon into warmed serving bowls, garnish with lemon slices and herb sprigs and serve.

Chinese lemon chicken

SERVES 6

Lemon chicken is a popular Cantonese dish of fried chicken glazed with a tart, lemony sauce. This homemade sauce is quite unlike the gluggy sauces often served with this dish.

500 g (1 lb 2 oz) boneless, skinless chicken
    breasts
1 tablespoon light soy sauce
1 tablespoon Chinese rice wine
1 spring onion (scallion), finely chopped
1 tablespoon finely chopped ginger
1 garlic clove, finely chopped
1 egg, lightly beaten
100 g (3 1/2 oz) cornflour (cornstarch)
oil, for deep-frying
steamed rice, to serve

lemon sauce
2 tablespoons lemon juice
2 teaspoons sugar
1/2 teaspoon sesame oil
3 tablespoons chicken stock
1/2 teaspoon cornflour (cornstarch)

Cut the chicken into slices. Place in a bowl, add the soy sauce, rice wine, spring onion, ginger and garlic and toss lightly. Marinate in the fridge for at least 1 hour, or overnight.

Add the egg to the chicken mixture and toss lightly to coat. Drain off the excess and coat the chicken pieces with the cornflour. The easiest way to do this is to put the chicken and cornflour in a plastic bag and shake it.

Fill a wok one-quarter full of oil and heat to 190°C (375°F), or until a cube of bread dropped into the oil turns golden brown in 10 seconds. Add half the chicken, a piece at a time, and deep-fry, stirring constantly, for 3–4 minutes, or until light golden brown. Remove with a wire sieve or slotted spoon and drain. Repeat with the remaining chicken.

Reheat the oil and return all the chicken to the wok. Cook until crisp and golden brown. Drain the chicken on paper towel. Pour off the oil and wipe out the wok.

To make the lemon sauce, combine the lemon juice, sugar, 1/2 teaspoon salt, sesame oil, stock and cornflour.

Reheat the wok over medium heat until hot, add the lemon sauce and stir constantly until the sauce is thickened. Add the chicken and toss lightly in the sauce. Serve immediately with steamed rice.

Preserved lemons

MAKES 2 LITRES (70 FL OZ/8 CUPS)

Preserved lemons are widely used in North African cooking
to flavour stews, tagines and couscous dishes, or to enhance
risottos, pastas and stuffings. This is a great way to use up
a glut of lemons and they will last for about 6 months.

8–12 small thin-skinned lemons
315 g (11 oz/1 cup) rock salt
750 ml (26 fl oz/3 cups) lemon juice
   (10–12 lemons)
1/2 teaspoon black peppercorns
1 bay leaf
olive oil

Scrub the lemons under warm running water
with a soft brush to remove the wax coating
if necessary.

Starting from the top and cutting almost to
the base, cut the lemons into quarters, taking
care not to cut all the way through. Gently
open each lemon, remove any visible seeds
and pack 1 tablespoon of the rock salt inside
each lemon.

Push the lemons back into shape and pack
tightly into a 2 litre (70 fl oz/8 cup) sterilised
jar (see notes) with a tight-fitting lid. The
lemons should be firmly packed and fill the
jar (depending on their size, you may not
need all 12 lemons).

Add 250 ml (9 fl oz/1 cup) of the lemon
juice, peppercorns, bay leaf and remaining
rock salt to the jar. Fill the jar to the top with
the remaining lemon juice. Seal and leave in
a cool, dark place for 6 weeks, inverting the
jar each week to dissolve the salt. The liquid

will be cloudy initially, but will clear by the
fourth week.

To test if the lemons are preserved, cut
through the centre of one of the lemon
quarters. If the pith is still white, the lemons
aren't quite ready. In this case, seal the jar
again and leave for another week before
testing again. The lemons should be
soft-skinned and the pith translucent.

Once the lemons are preserved, cover the
brine with a layer of olive oil. Replace the oil
each time you remove some of the lemon
pieces, so the lemons remain covered with
oil. Refrigerate after opening.

notes When using preserved lemons in
cooking, use only the peel (the zest) and not
the flesh. Discard the salty flesh and bitter
pith, then rinse and thinly slice or chop the
zest and use as directed.

Jars must always be sterilised before pickles,
preserves or jams are put in them for storage,
otherwise bacteria will multiply. To sterilise
jars and lids, rinse them with boiling water
and place in a warm oven for 20 minutes,
or until completely dry. (Jars with rubber
seals are safe to warm in the oven and won't
melt.) Never dry your jars with a tea towel
— even a clean one may have germs on it
and will contaminate the jars.

lime

There could be nothing more refreshing than the smell of a just-cut lime. We use their piquant juice to flavour drinks such as margaritas, mojitos and daiquiris; in dishes such as guacamole and salsa; we squeeze their fresh juice over chunks of low–acid tropical fruits such as papaya and mango to add a bit of zing; and we use them in the legendary key lime pie.

Varieties

Key lime The West Indian or key lime is considered to be the 'true' lime. This golf-ball small lime has highly acidic, intensely flavoured, juicy flesh. It's difficult to find it outside of the Florida Keys area in the United States, from where it got its name.

Tahitian (or Persian) This is the most commonly found lime, thought to be a hybrid of the true lime. It is seedless and thin-skinned, and has pale, juicy flesh.

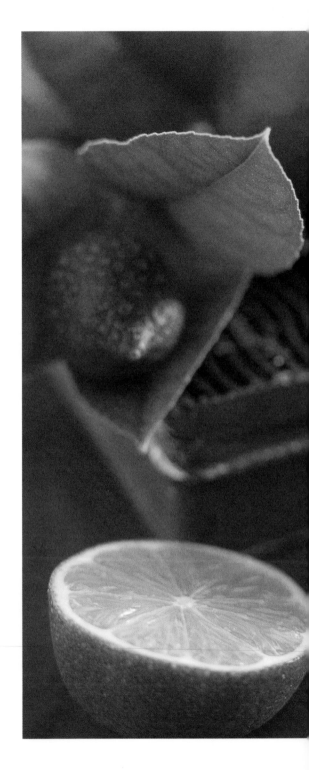

Kaffir Found throughout Southeast Asia, these limes have thick bumpy skin, highly aromatic and uniquely double-shaped leaves and very little juice. Kaffirs are not strictly limes but are a citrus subspecies. The word 'kaffir' is Arabic for 'infidel' and has racist connotations in South Africa, so the fruit may also be found by the Thai name, makrut. Finely grated or shredded, both the leaves and zest are used in cooking, while the bitter juice and flesh are rarely used.

Buying and storing

- The peak season for limes is from autumn to early winter.

- Limes are green because they are picked and sold while still unripe, as this is when their flavour is best. When fully ripe, their skin turns yellow and they lose their hallmark fragrant acidity. Buy firm limes that are darkish green in colour and glossy-skinned.

- Store in the fridge for up to 2 weeks, or for 1 week at cool room temperature. Lime juice and grated zest can be frozen for 3 months.

Preparation

To make the juice easier to extract, put the limes in a bowl of hot water for 1 minute. Drain and cool, then roll the lime with the palm of your hand on a hard surface. Halve and squeeze the juice. Limes can be used interchangeably with lemons, but because their flavour is more assertive than lemon you will need to use less.

Don't cook limes in aluminium or iron cookware, as the acids will react with the metal, causing changes in the colour and taste of your food.

To chop fresh kaffir lime leaves, stack two or three leaves in a pile. Roll the leaves from tip to stem into a bundle, then thinly slice, discarding the tough central stem.

Key lime pie

SERVES 6–8

sweet shortcrust pastry
250 g (9 oz/2 cups) plain (all-purpose) flour
125 g (4^1/$_2$ oz) cold unsalted butter, chopped
2 tablespoons caster (superfine) sugar
2–3 tablespoons iced water

filling
4 egg yolks
400 g (14 oz) tin sweetened condensed milk
125 ml (4 fl oz/^{1}/$_2$ cup) lime juice
2 teaspoons finely grated lime zest
lime slices, to garnish
icing (confectioners') sugar, to dust
whipped cream, to serve

Sift the flour and ^{1}/$_4$ teaspoon salt into a large bowl. Using your fingertips, lightly rub in the butter until the mixture resembles breadcrumbs. Fold in the sugar. Make a well in the centre and gradually add most of the iced water, mixing with a flat-bladed knife. The mixture will come together in small beads of dough. If necessary, add more water, a teaspoon at a time, until the dough comes together. Test the dough by pinching a little piece between your fingers — if it doesn't hold together, it needs more water.

Gather the dough together and lift out onto a lightly floured surface. Press the dough into a ball and then flatten slightly. Cover in plastic wrap and refrigerate for 20–30 minutes.

Preheat the oven to 180°C (350°F/Gas 4). Grease a 23 cm (9 inch) loose-based tart tin. Roll the dough out between two sheets of baking paper until it is large enough to fit into the tin. Remove the top sheet of paper and invert the pastry into the tin. Use a small ball of dough to help press the pastry into the tin, allowing any excess to hang over the side. Trim off the excess pastry.

Line the pastry shell with baking paper and pour in some baking beads or rice. Bake for 10 minutes, then remove the paper and beads and return the pastry to the oven for a further 5 minutes, or until the base is dry to touch. Leave to cool.

To make the filling, use electric beaters to beat the egg yolks, condensed milk, lime juice and zest in a large bowl for 2 minutes, or until well combined. Pour into the pastry shell and smooth the surface. Bake for 20–25 minutes, or until set. Allow the pie to cool, then refrigerate for 2 hours, or until well chilled. Garnish with lime slices, dust with sifted icing sugar and serve with cream.

note This famous American pie is made from the limes that grow in the Florida Keys area. The traditional version uses egg whites in the filling and is topped with meringue. Unlike most limes, key lime juice is pale yellow, so some cooks add green food colouring to exaggerate the lime colour; a practice frowned upon by key lime pie aficionados.

Thom kha gai soup

SERVES 4

750 ml (26 fl oz/3 cups) coconut milk
2 lemongrass stems, white part only, bruised
5 cm (2 inch) piece galangal, peeled and
    cut into several pieces
4 red Asian shallots, peeled and crushed
    with the flat side of a knife
400 g (14 oz) boneless, skinless chicken
    breasts, thinly sliced
2 tablespoons fish sauce
1 tablespoon grated palm sugar (jaggery)
200 g (7 oz) cherry tomatoes, halved
150 g (5½ oz) straw mushrooms or
    button mushrooms
3 tablespoons lime juice
6 kaffir (makrut) lime leaves, torn in half
3–5 bird's eye chillies, stems removed,
    bruised, or 2 long red chillies, seeded
    and thinly sliced
coriander (cilantro) leaves, to garnish

Put the coconut milk, lemongrass, galangal and shallots in a saucepan or wok over medium heat and bring to the boil.

Add the chicken, fish sauce and palm sugar and simmer, stirring constantly, for 5 minutes, or until the chicken is cooked through.

Add the tomatoes and mushrooms and simmer for 2–3 minutes, then add the lime juice, lime leaves and chillies in the last few seconds, taking care not to let the tomatoes lose their shape. Taste, then adjust the seasoning if necessary. Serve garnished with coriander leaves.

note This soup is one of the classic dishes of Thailand. It translates literally as 'boiled galangal chicken' — which doesn't really do justice to its perfect blend of hot, sour, sweet and salty. You can make this with prawns or fish instead of chicken. Don't worry when the coconut milk splits; it's supposed to.

Lime juice is very useful in meat marinades as it has a natural tenderising effect; it will actually 'cook' the diced flesh of fresh fish and other tender seafoods when used in quantity.

Lime marmalade

MAKES 2.25 LITRES (79 FL OZ/9 CUPS)

1 kg (2 lb 4 oz) limes
10 cm (4 inch) square of muslin
  (cheesecloth)
2.25 kg (5 lb/10¼ cups) sugar

Scrub the limes under warm running water to remove any wax.

Cut the fruit in half lengthways, reserving any seeds. Slice the fruit very thinly and place in a large non-metallic bowl along with 2 litres (70 fl oz/8 cups) water. Tie any seeds securely in the muslin and add to the bowl. Cover and leave overnight.

Put two small plates in the freezer. Put the fruit, water and muslin bag in a large saucepan. Bring slowly to the boil, then reduce the heat and simmer, covered, for 30–45 minutes, or until the fruit is tender.

Meanwhile, warm the sugar slightly by first spreading it in a large baking tin and then heating it in a 120°C (235°F/Gas ½) oven for 10 minutes, stirring occasionally. Do not add the sugar to the jam until the fruit has softened. If the sugar is added before the fruit has fully softened, the fruit will stay firm.

Add the warmed sugar to the pan and stir over low heat, without boiling, for 5 minutes, or until dissolved. Return to the boil and boil rapidly, stirring often, for 20 minutes. Using a slotted spoon, remove any scum from the surface of the jam during cooking. When the syrup falls from a wooden spoon in thick sheets, test for setting point.

To do this, remove the pan from the heat, put a little marmalade onto one of the cold plates and return the plate to the freezer for 30 seconds. A skin should form on the surface and the marmalade should wrinkle when pushed with your finger. If not, return the pan to the heat and retest a few minutes later with the other plate. When the jam is cooked, discard the muslin bag.

Transfer the marmalade to a heatproof jug and immediately pour into hot sterilised jars (see page 24), and seal. Turn the jars upside down for 2 minutes, then turn back up again and leave to cool completely. Label and date for storage.

Store in a cool, dark place for 6–12 months. Once opened, the marmalade will keep in the refrigerator for 8 weeks.

As a useful guide, 1 **lime** will yield about 40 ml (1¼ fl oz/2 tablespoons) of juice and 1½ teaspoons of finely grated zest.

mandarin & tangerine

Mandarins are one of the three original species of citrus (along with pomelos and citrons), and all other citrus fruit are hybrids or mutations of these, including tangerines. Mandarin trees are native to China, where they have been cultivated for thousands of years. There the fruit was once reserved exclusively for the privileged classes, or Mandarins — possibly how the fruit acquired its name. Tangerines were so-named because they were first imported into Europe through the port city of Tangiers in Morocco.

Varieties

Clementine Discovered by Father Clément Rodier in Algeria in the early 1900s, the clementine is a cross between a mandarin and a bitter seville orange. Clementines have juicy flesh — some varieties are virtually seedless — and loose, smooth easy-to-peel skin.

Honey mandarin These are classified as a tangerine and are called murcott in some countries. A cross between a mandarin and sweet orange hybrids, these are thin-skinned and have a smooth, shiny skin and very sweet, juicy flesh.

Satsuma The satsuma originated in Japan and there are over 70 varieties. Most are seedless and have loose, easily removed skin and highly perfumed sweet–sour flesh.

Tangelo A cross between a mandarin and either a grapefruit or pomelo, tangelos are similar in size and colour to an orange but are distinguished by a characteristic nipple at the stem end (pictured far left). They have easy-to-peel bright orange skin and very juicy flesh.

Tangor A cross between a mandarin and a sweet orange, the tangor is a largish fruit with sweet, perfumed, juicy flesh.

Buying and storing

- Mandarins are in season from autumn to late spring, and tangerines are in season in winter.

- Mandarins can dry out quickly, so buy fruit that are heavy for their size, and ask if you can try before you buy.

- Don't buy mandarins with overly puffy skin, as these are probably overripe.

- Mandarins don't keep as well as other citrus. Store them in the fridge for up to 10 days, or up to 1 week at cool room temperature.

Chilled mandarin soufflé

SERVES 4

5 eggs, separated
230 g (8 oz/1 cup) caster (superfine) sugar
2 teaspoons finely grated mandarin zest
185 ml (6 fl oz/^{3}/4 cup) strained mandarin
    juice
1 tablespoon powdered gelatine
310 ml (10^3/4 fl oz/1 ^{1}/4 cups) cream, lightly
    whipped, plus extra to serve
julienned mandarin zest, to garnish

Cut out four wide strips of foil, then fold each in half lengthways. Wrap the foil strips around the outside of four 250 ml (9 fl oz/1 cup) soufflé dishes, positioning the foil so that it extends 4 cm (1^1/2 inches) above the rims. Secure with string. Brush the inside of the foil with a little oil.

In a small bowl, beat the egg yolks, sugar and mandarin zest using electric beaters for 3 minutes, or until the sugar has dissolved and the mixture is thick and pale.

Heat the mandarin juice in a small saucepan. Whisking continuously, gradually add the juice to the egg yolk mixture until well combined.

Sprinkle the gelatine over 3 tablespoons water in a small heatproof bowl, then leave to stand for 5 minutes, or until the gelatine is soft. Stand the bowl in a small saucepan of barely simmering water and heat for 3 minutes, or until the gelatine has dissolved. Gradually add the gelatine to the mandarin mixture, whisking gently until combined.

Transfer to a large bowl, cover with plastic wrap and refrigerate for 15 minutes, or until the mixture has thickened but has not set. Using a metal spoon, gently fold the whipped cream into the mandarin mixture until almost combined.

Using electric beaters, whisk the egg whites in a clean, dry bowl until soft peaks form. Fold the beaten egg white quickly and lightly into the mandarin mixture until the mixture is just combined, with no streaks of egg white remaining. Gently spoon into the prepared soufflé dishes and refrigerate for 4 hours, or until set.

To serve, remove the foil collars, then decorate with whipped cream and julienned mandarin zest.

note This chilled soufflé can be made up to 8 hours ahead of serving.

Mandarin juice can be used as a flavoursome alternative to orange juice. Use their grated zest and juice in recipes that call for orange and enjoy the fragrant difference.

Mandarin soda

MAKES 500 ML (17 FL OZ/2 CUPS) SYRUP

250 g (9 oz/heaped 1 cup) sugar
375 ml (13 fl oz/1 1/2 cups) mandarin juice
soda water or sparkling mineral water,
    to serve
ice cubes, to serve

Put the sugar and 600 ml (21 fl oz/2 1/2 cups) water in a saucepan over low heat, stirring occasionally until the sugar has dissolved. Bring to the boil and cook for 5 minutes.

Add the mandarin juice and boil for a further 5 minutes. Allow to cool, then pour into a hot sterilised airtight jar (see page 24) and refrigerate for 1 hour. Use 2–3 tablespoons of syrup per glass and top up with soda or sparkling mineral water and ice cubes.

Tangerine gelato

SERVES 6

5 egg yolks
115 g (4 oz/1/2 cup) sugar
500 ml (17 fl oz/2 cups) milk
2 tablespoons finely grated tangerine zest
185 ml (6 fl oz/3/4 cup) tangerine juice
3 tablespoons thick (double/heavy) cream

Using electric beaters, whisk the egg yolks and half the sugar together until pale and creamy. Put the milk, tangerine zest and remaining sugar in a saucepan and bring to the boil, stirring to dissolve the sugar.

Pour a little of the milk mixture over the egg mixture and whisk to combine, then pour in the remaining milk, whisking constantly. Pour the custard back into the saucepan and cook over low heat, stirring continuously, until the mixture is thick enough to coat the back of a wooden spoon — do not allow the custard to boil.

Strain the custard into a bowl, add the tangerine juice and cream and then cool over ice. When cool, churn in an ice-cream maker following the manufacturer's instructions. Alternatively, pour into a plastic freezer box, cover and freeze. Stir every 30 minutes with a whisk during freezing to break up the ice crystals and give a better texture. Keep in the freezer until ready to serve.

orange

Oranges travel well and thanks to a year-round supply we almost take them for granted. We use them with sophistication in the French duck à l'orange and crepes suzette; we start our day with a glass of freshly squeezed, vitamin-rich juice; we cook them whole in cakes; grate their fragrant zest into fruitcake batters; and use their sweet juice to make refreshing sorbets and granitas. Although we tend to associate the word 'orange' with the fruit's colour, it actually refers to the fruit's aroma — its name comes from the Sanskrit word *naranga*, meaning 'fragrant'.

Varieties

Oranges can be roughly divided into two groups: bitter and sweet. Bitter oranges, such as sevilles and bergamots, are used in general cooking, in marmalades or used for their zest. Sweet oranges, such as navels, valencias and blood oranges, are eaten as a fresh fruit, added to salads and used for their juice.

Navel Characterised by a navel-like depression on its base, the popular navel orange has bright orange, slightly pebbly skin, and juicy, sweet flesh, which is almost always seedless.

Valencia This large fruit has more seeds than a navel orange and often has a green-tinged skin. Oranges need a cool temperature to retain their orange skin colour and valencias harvested in summer may lose some colour as a result. The valencia is ideal for juicing.

Seville A thick-skinned bitter orange with lots of seeds, the seville is used as a cooking orange for savoury recipes requiring orange juice, and for marmalade. Their peel is often candied and their essential oils are used to make the liqueurs Grand Marnier, Cointreau and Curaçao. In the Middle East, the blossoms of bitter oranges are used to make fragrant orange-flower water.

Blood orange These sweet and richly flavoured oranges have lots of red pigmentation, which varies depending on growing conditions — those grown in cooler climates seem to be redder than those from warmer areas. They have a spicy, almost berried flavour and are good in salads, fresh drinks and the French sauce, maltaise (a derivative of hollandaise sauce). Their season is short.

Buying and storing

- Oranges are available year-round but their peak season is in winter.

- Oranges should feel heavy with juice for their size, have tight skin and give when gentle pressure is applied. They should not be shrivelled or bruised and should have no soft spongy spots.

- Store oranges at room temperature for 3 days, or in a loosely sealed plastic bag in the crisper of the fridge for up to 2 weeks.

Preparation

Segmenting To segment an orange, cut a thin slice from each end of the orange, then put the orange, flat side down, on the cutting board. Working from the top of the orange to the base and following the curve of the fruit, slice off the skin and bitter pith in strips. Then, holding the orange over a bowl to catch the juices, cut between the white membranes to remove the segments. Squeeze the leftover membranes to extract any juice, then discard them.

Zesting If a recipe asks for orange zest, this can be removed from the orange using a zester or using the fine holes of a grater; either way, it is important to remove as little of the bitter white pith as possible. Use a pastry brush to brush all the loose bits from inside and outside the grater. If using the zest in a sweet dish, rub a sugar cube over the orange before grating it to extract the oils.

For julienned zest, use a knife or vegetable peeler to slice off pieces of orange zest, then cut it into fine strips and use as decoration. Blanch the strips to make them more tender, if you prefer.

Candied orange zest Strips of candied orange (or any citrus) zest make excellent — and perfectly edible — decorations for cakes and cheesecakes. Remove the zest from 3 oranges and cut into julienne strips. Put the zest in a saucepan with a little water and bring to the boil. Simmer for 1 minute, then drain the water and repeat the boiling process. This will get rid of any bitterness in the zest and syrup.

Drain, then put 220 g (7¾ oz/1 cup) sugar and 3 tablespoons water in the pan and stir until the sugar has dissolved. Add the zest and bring to the boil, then reduce the heat and simmer for 5–6 minutes, or until the zest looks translucent — don't overcook or it will caramelise. Drain the zest and dry on baking paper (you can use the syrup to drizzle over the cake if you like).

Oranges go well with ingredients such as chocolate, almonds, walnuts, liqueurs, Marsala, duck liver, cumin, ginger, cardamom, chillies, prawns (shrimp), pork, mint, olives, carrot, spinach and beetroot.

Ricotta crepes with orange sauce

SERVES 4

85 g (3 oz/^{2}/$_3$ cup) plain (all-purpose) flour
1 egg, lightly beaten
330 ml (11 ^{1}/$_4$ fl oz/1 ^{1}/$_3$ cups) milk
butter, for cooking

filling

3 tablespoons sultanas (golden raisins)
250 ml (9 fl oz/1 cup) orange juice
200 g (7 oz/heaped ^{3}/$_4$ cup) ricotta cheese
1 teaspoon finely grated orange zest
^{1}/$_4$ teaspoon natural vanilla extract

orange sauce

50 g (1 ^{3}/$_4$ oz) unsalted butter
3 tablespoons caster (superfine) sugar
1 tablespoon orange liqueur, such as
    Grand Marnier

Sift the flour and a pinch of salt into a bowl and make a well in the centre. In another bowl, combine the egg and milk, then add to the well in the flour and beat using a wire whisk until a smooth batter forms. Cover with plastic wrap and set aside for 30 minutes.

Heat a 16 cm (6 ^{1}/$_4$ inch) crepe or non-stick frying pan. Lightly grease with butter, then pour 2–3 tablespoons of batter into the pan, swirling the pan so the mixture coats the base evenly. Cook over medium heat for 1–2 minutes, or until golden underneath. Turn and cook the other side for 30 seconds, then transfer to a plate. Repeat with the remaining batter to make eight crepes, greasing the pan lightly as needed and stacking the crepes on a plate, with a sheet of baking paper between each crepe.

Preheat the oven to 160°C (315°F/Gas 2–3).

To make the filling, put the sultanas in a small bowl, pour the orange juice over and leave to soak for 15 minutes. Drain the sultanas well, reserving the orange juice, and place in a larger bowl along with the ricotta, orange zest and vanilla. Mix together well.

Place large tablespoons of the filling at the edge of each crepe. Fold the crepe in half, then in half again. Arrange two crepes on each of four ovenproof serving plates and bake for 10 minutes.

Meanwhile, make the orange sauce. Melt the butter in a small saucepan over low heat. Add the sugar and reserved orange juice and stir over medium heat, without boiling, until the sugar has dissolved. Bring to the boil, then reduce the heat and simmer for 10 minutes, or until reduced slightly. Stir in the liqueur and allow to cool for 3–4 minutes.

Pour the orange sauce over the warm crepes and serve immediately.

note The crepes can be cooked up to 4 hours in advance. Cover and refrigerate until required, then fill and heat them in the oven just before serving.

Orange poppy seed cake

SERVES 8–10

185 g (6$\frac{1}{2}$ oz) unsalted butter, softened
170 g (6 oz/$\frac{3}{4}$ cup) caster (superfine) sugar
3 eggs
1 teaspoon natural vanilla extract
2$\frac{1}{2}$ tablespoons poppy seeds
1 teaspoon finely grated orange zest
185 g (6$\frac{1}{2}$ oz/1$\frac{1}{2}$ cups) self-raising flour
60 g (2$\frac{1}{4}$ oz/$\frac{1}{2}$ cup) plain (all-purpose)
   flour
3 tablespoons milk

candied citrus
2 oranges
2 lemons
500 g (1 lb 2 oz) caster (superfine) sugar

Preheat the oven to 180°C (350°F/Gas 4).
Grease a 22 cm (8$\frac{1}{2}$ inch) round cake tin
or kugelhopf tin and lightly dust with flour,
shaking out any excess.

Using electric beaters, cream the butter and
sugar until light and fluffy. Add the eggs one
at a time, beating well after each addition.
Add the vanilla, poppy seeds and orange zest
and stir until well combined.

Sift the flours into a bowl. Using a large metal
spoon, gently fold the flour into the butter
mixture, alternating with the milk, until just
combined and almost smooth.

Spoon the batter into the prepared cake
tin and smooth over the surface. Bake for
45 minutes, or until a skewer inserted into
the centre of the cake comes out clean.
Remove from the oven, leave in the tin for
10 minutes, then turn out onto a wire cake
rack to cool slightly.

While the cake is baking, prepare the candied
citrus. Cut the oranges and lemons into slices
about 4 mm ($\frac{1}{8}$ inch) thick. Place 250 g
(9 oz) of the sugar in a heavy-based frying
pan with 4 tablespoons water. Stir over low
heat until the sugar has completely dissolved.
Bring to the boil, then reduce the heat and
simmer. Add a quarter of the fruit slices to
the syrup and simmer for 5–10 minutes, or
until the fruit is transparent and the syrup is
reduced and toffee-like. Lift out the fruit with
tongs and cool on a wire rack.

Add 80 g (2$\frac{3}{4}$ oz/$\frac{1}{3}$ cup) of the remaining
sugar to the syrup and stir to dissolve.
Simmer a second batch of fruit slices in the
syrup as before, then remove. Add another
80 g (2$\frac{3}{4}$ oz/$\frac{1}{3}$ cup) sugar to the syrup and
stir to dissolve, then simmer a third batch of
fruit slices in the syrup, then remove. Repeat
with the remaining sugar and fruit slices.
Reserve the syrup and allow the candied
citrus slices to firm.

Place the warm cake, still on the wire rack,
over a tray. Pierce all over with a skewer,
then pour the hot syrup over, allowing it to
soak in — if the syrup is too thick, thin it with
a little orange juice. Set the cake on a serving
plate and arrange some of the firm candied
citrus slices over the top.

Serve within a few hours of decorating. Any
leftover candied citrus can be kept between
layers of baking paper in an airtight container
for up to 2 days.

Roasted fennel and orange salad

SERVES 4

8 baby fennel bulbs
100 ml (3 1/2 fl oz) olive oil
2 oranges
1 tablespoon lemon juice
1 red onion, halved and thinly sliced
100 g (3 1/2 oz) kalamata olives
2 tablespoons roughly chopped mint
1 tablespoon roughly chopped parsley

Preheat the oven to 200°C (400°F/Gas 6). Trim the fronds from the fennel bulbs and reserve. Remove the stalks and cut a 5 mm (1/4 inch) slice off the base of each fennel. Slice each fennel into 6 wedges, place in a baking dish and drizzle with 3 tablespoons of the olive oil. Season well with salt and pepper, then bake for 40–45 minutes, or until the fennel is tender and slightly caramelised. Turn once or twice during cooking. Allow to cool.

Cut a thin slice off the top and bottom of each orange. Using a small sharp knife and following the curve of the fruit, slice off the skin and bitter pith. Holding the orange over a bowl to catch the juices, cut between the white membranes to remove the segments. Squeeze the leftover membranes to extract any juice, then discard them.

Add the lemon juice to the orange juice in the bowl, then whisk in the remaining oil until emulsified. Season well. Combine the orange segments, onion and olives in a bowl, pour on half the dressing and add half the mint. Mix well, then transfer to a serving dish. Top with the roasted fennel, drizzle with the remaining dressing and scatter the parsley and remaining mint over the top. Chop the reserved fronds and sprinkle over the salad.

Orange hollandaise sauce

MAKES 300 ML (10 1/2 FL OZ)

175 g (6 oz) butter
4 egg yolks
2 tablespoons orange juice
ground white pepper

Melt the butter in a small saucepan. Skim any foam from the top of the butter and discard. Set the melted butter aside to cool.

Combine 2 tablespoons water and the egg yolks in a separate saucepan. Whisk for about 30 seconds, or until the mixture is pale and creamy. Put the pan over very low heat and continue whisking for 3 minutes, or until thick and foamy, then remove from the heat. (Make sure the saucepan does not get too hot or you will end up with scrambled eggs.)

Add the cooled butter slowly, a little at a time at first, whisking well after each addition. Keep adding the butter in a thin stream, whisking continuously, until all the butter has been used. Try to avoid using the milky white whey in the bottom of the pan, but don't worry if a little gets in. Stir in the orange juice and season with salt and white pepper.

Serve over steamed asparagus or with salmon steaks or other seafood.

variation To make a basic hollandaise sauce replace the 2 tablespoons orange juice with 1 tablespoon lemon juice. (Strain the juice through a fine sieve to remove any pulp before measuring.)

Orange, hazelnut and goat's cheese salad

SERVES 4

35 g (1¼ oz/¼ cup) hazelnuts
1 tablespoon orange juice
1 tablespoon lemon juice
125 ml (4 fl oz/½ cup) olive oil
250 g (9 oz) watercress
50 g (1¾ oz/1 cup) baby English spinach
    leaves
24 orange segments (about 2 oranges)
300 g (10½ oz) firm goat's cheese, sliced
    into 4 equal portions

Preheat the oven to 180°C (350°F/Gas 4). Put the hazelnuts on a tray and roast for 5–6 minutes, or until the skins turn dark brown. Wrap the hazelnuts in a clean tea towel and rub them together to remove the skins. You won't be able to remove all the skins but most should easily rub off.

To make the dressing, combine the nuts, orange juice, lemon juice and a pinch of salt in a food processor. With the motor running, gradually add the olive oil, a few drops at a time. When about half the oil has been added, pour in the remainder in a steady stream.

Remove the stems from the watercress and place the leaves in a bowl along with the spinach, orange segments and 2 tablespoons of the dressing. Toss to combine and season with sea salt and freshly ground black pepper. Arrange the salad on four plates.

Heat a small non-stick frying pan over medium–high heat and brush lightly with olive oil. When hot, carefully press each slice of goat's cheese firmly into the pan and cook for 1–2 minutes, or until a crust has formed on the cheese. Carefully remove the cheese from the pan and arrange over the salads, crust side up. Before serving, drizzle over the remaining dressing.

One single **orange** contains more than 100 per cent of the recommended daily intake of vitamin C. Oranges also contain vitamin A, dietary fibre, thiamine, folate, potassium, antioxidants and even a little protein. They aid the body in healing, absorbing iron and in boosting immunity.

Orange and almond cake

SERVES 8–10

2 large oranges
5 eggs
250 g (9 oz/2 1/2 cups) ground almonds
220 g (7 3/4 oz/1 cup) sugar
1 teaspoon baking powder
icing (confectioners') sugar, to dust

Grease a 22 cm (8 1/2 inch) spring-form cake tin and line the base with baking paper.

Scrub the oranges under warm running water to remove any wax coating from the skins. Put the whole oranges in a saucepan, cover with water and boil for 1 hour. Remove from the water and set aside to cool.

Preheat the oven to 180°C (350°F/Gas 4). Using a plate to catch any juice, cut the cooled oranges into quarters and remove any seeds. Blend the orange quarters, including the skin, in a food processor or blender until they turn to a pulp.

Beat the eggs in a large bowl with electric beaters until light and fluffy. Add the orange pulp and any reserved juice to the bowl along with the almonds, sugar and baking powder. Mix thoroughly to combine.

Pour the batter into the prepared tin. Bake for 1 hour, or until the cake is firm to touch and lightly golden. Cook the cake a little longer if it is still wet. Remove from the oven, leave in the tin for 10 minutes, then turn out onto a wire cake rack to cool. Dust with sifted icing sugar before serving.

Seville marmalade was invented in Scotland in the 1700s, quite by accident. A Spanish ship took refuge in Dundee harbour and its load of **oranges** was bought by a local. He discovered them to be too bitter to eat so his wife turned them into a sweetened preserve.

Blood orange mayonnaise

MAKES 150 ML (5 FL OZ)

1 egg yolk
1 teaspoon white wine vinegar
1/2 teaspoon dijon mustard
125 ml (4 fl oz/1/2 cup) olive oil
2 tablespoons blood orange juice

To make the blood orange mayonnaise, whisk together the egg yolk, white wine vinegar and dijon mustard. Whisking constantly, gradually drizzle in the olive oil until you have a thick emulsion. Mix through the blood orange juice, to taste. Season with sea salt and freshly ground black pepper.

Three-fruit marmalade

MAKES 2.25 LITRES (79 FL OZ/9 CUPS)

1 grapefruit
2 oranges
2 lemons
10 cm (4 inch) square of muslin
    (cheesecloth)
3 kg (6 lb 12 oz) sugar

Scrub the grapefruit, oranges and lemons under warm running water with a soft brush to remove any wax coating.

Cut the grapefruit into quarters, and the oranges and lemons in half. Slice the fruit very thinly, reserving any seeds, and place the fruit slices in a large non-metallic bowl with 2.5 litres (87 fl oz/10 cups) water. Tie any seeds securely in the muslin and add to the bowl. Cover and leave overnight.

Put two small plates in the freezer. Put the fruit, water and muslin bag in a large heavy-based saucepan. Bring slowly to the boil, then reduce the heat and simmer, covered, for 1 hour, or until the fruit is tender.

Meanwhile, warm the sugar slightly by first spreading it in a large baking tin and then heating it in a 120°C (235°F/Gas $^1/_2$) oven for 10 minutes, stirring occasionally.

Add the warmed sugar to the fruit all at once. Stir over low heat, without boiling, for 5 minutes, or until the sugar has dissolved. Bring the mixture to the boil, then boil rapidly for 50–60 minutes. When the syrup falls from a wooden spoon in thick sheets, test for setting point.

To do this, remove the pan from the heat. Put a little of the hot marmalade onto one of the cold plates and return the plate to the freezer for 30 seconds. When setting point is reached, a skin should form on the surface and the marmalade should wrinkle when pushed with your finger. If not, return the pan to the heat and retest a few minutes later with the other plate. Leave to cool for 10 minutes, then skim off any impurities that have risen to the surface. Remove the muslin bag.

Transfer the marmalade to a heatproof jug and immediately pour into hot sterilised jars (see page 24), and seal. Turn the jars upside down for 2 minutes, then turn back up again and leave to cool. Label and date for storage.

Store in a cool, dark place for 12 months. Once opened, the marmalade will keep in the fridge for 8 weeks.

hard fruit

apple

Apples are one of the earliest cultivated fruits, and all modern-day varieties can trace their roots back to the earliest form of apple, the wild crab apple that originated in the Caucasian mountains, in Kazakhstan. Today there are around 8000 named apple varieties, but only a proportion of these are grown commercially, mainly for their uniformity in size and shape, their ability to travel well and their resistance to disease.

Varieties

Apples are generally grouped as either cooking or eating apples, and some fall into both groups. Good eating apples have a crisp, firm texture and a high sugar content, with some acidity to counterbalance their sweetness. These apples hold their shape well and are perfect for use in pies and tarts. Good eating apples include red delicious, braeburn, royal gala and lady william.

Apples suited for cooking, such as those used to make purées or crumbles, are more acidic and become soft when baked or stewed. Some apples are good for both cooking and eating raw, and include golden delicious, cox's orange pippin, granny smith, pink lady and johnathon. Cooking apples such as the acidic green-skinned British bramley and newton wonders are usually very sour and are best used as cooking apples.

Braeburn This firm, juicy apple has red-blushed skin and a delicate sweet–sour flavour. It is best suited for eating raw or adding to salads. This variety is at its best at the start of the apple season, from autumn to early winter.

Fuji Originally from Japan and named after Mount Fuji, these reddish pink apples have juicy, crisp flesh and a high sugar content, which makes them one of the sweetest of all the cultivated apples, and the perfect eating apple. Because they hold their texture well, they are also suited to baking whole and adding to pies. Fujis are a late season variety.

Pink lady This is one of the newest apple varieties and was first grown in 1979 in Western Australia. It is a cross between the golden delicious and lady william apples. With pink-blushed skin and crisp, juicy, sweet flesh, these apples are great for both eating and cooking. They have a unique sugar-acid balance, so are ideal for baking whole and using in pies. Pink ladies are a late season apple.

Cox's orange pippin Created by Englishman Richard Cox in 1825, this English apple variety is generally small and round, with greenish yellow skin flushed with some red. This sweet, juicy apple has a crisp, firm texture. While it is an all-purpose apple, it is best eaten out of hand and is at its peak in autumn.

Red delicious First discovered in 1880 in Iowa, this slightly elongated apple has thick, tough, deep red skin and distinct ridged bumps at its base. With crisp, juicy white flesh and a low level of acidity, red delicious is a good eating apple, but is not suited for cooking at all. These apples are best bought in the winter months.

Golden delicious Discovered in West Virginia in 1914, this apple has yellowy green skin and tender sweet flesh. Although it shares part of its name with the red delicious, they are related in name only. Golden delicious holds its shape without emitting too much moisture, making it perfect for caramelised apple desserts, tarts and pies, but it is also a good eating apple. This variety is in season throughout winter.

Granny smith This apple variety is named after Australian Maria Ann Smith ('granny' Smith), who found the seedlings growing in a spot in her Sydney garden, where she had thrown some apple cores. These apples have thick, freckled, apple-green skin and crisp, tart white flesh. This variety is suitable for both eating and cooking. As its flesh collapses when cooked, it is a good variety for purées and sauces.

Buying and storing

- Apples are in season from autumn to winter; the different varieties appear during different times of the season.

- Apples out of season may be floury and lacking in flavour as these have been kept in cold storage. Buy apple varieties from your grower's market as they come into their peak season. You'll also be able to try them before you buy them, and you may discover a few new ones.

- Buy firm, smooth and shiny-skinned apples that feel heavy for their size. Apples should still have their stalks intact and have dry, tight skin.

- Apples store well at room temperature, but will maintain their crisp texture for longer if stored in a ventilated plastic bag in the crisper of the fridge, where they will keep for up to 1 week.

Preparation

Put peeled and cut apples in a bowl of water with lemon juice added (acidulated water), or lightly brush with lemon juice to prevent them from browning.

If coring quantities of apples, a purpose-made apple corer can be purchased for the job.

Traditional apple sauce

SERVES 6–8

4 green apples, peeled, cored and chopped
2 teaspoons caster (superfine) sugar
2 cloves
1 cinnamon stick
1–2 teaspoons lemon juice

Put the apples, sugar, cloves, cinnamon stick and 125 ml (4 fl oz/$1/2$ cup) water in a small saucepan. Cover and simmer over low heat for 10 minutes, or until the apple is soft. Remove from the heat and discard the cloves and cinnamon stick.

Mash the apple, or press through a sieve for a smooth-textured sauce. Stir in the lemon juice, to taste.

Serve the apple sauce warm or cold with roast pork, pork chops or pan-fried pork fillet. The apple sauce will keep for up to 4 days stored in the fridge.

Chicken stew with apple potato mash

SERVES 4

1 kg (2 lb 4 oz) boneless, skinless chicken
    thighs, cut into 2 cm ($3/4$ inch) cubes
$1^{1}/2$ tablespoons finely chopped thyme
1 tablespoon oil
90 g ($3^{1}/4$ oz) butter
3 French shallots, thinly sliced
375 ml (13 fl oz/$1^{1}/2$ cups) apple cider
1 kg (2 lb 4 oz) all-purpose potatoes, cubed
2 large green apples, peeled, cored and cut
    into eighths
170 ml ($5^{1}/2$ fl oz/$2/3$ cup) cream

Season the chicken with 2 teaspoons of the thyme and some salt and pepper. Heat the oil and 20 g ($3/4$ oz) of the butter in a large saucepan over medium–high heat. Cook the chicken in two batches for 2–3 minutes, or until evenly browned. Remove from the pan.

Add the shallots and remaining thyme to the pan and sauté for 2 minutes. Add the cider, then bring to the boil, stirring well. Return the chicken to the pan, cover, then reduce the heat to medium–low and cook for about 35 minutes, or until the chicken is tender and the sauce has reduced (check occasionally to see if any water needs to be added).

Cook the potatoes and apples in a saucepan of boiling water for 15–20 minutes, or until tender. Drain and return to the pan over low heat for 1 minute to evaporate any water, then mash. Stir in 2 tablespoons of cream and the remaining butter with a wooden spoon, then season with salt and pepper.

Stir the remaining cream into the chicken stew and cook for 2–4 minutes to thicken. Serve with the potato and apple mash.

Leek, taleggio and apple risotto

SERVES 6

1.25 litres (44 fl oz/5 cups) chicken
    or vegetable stock
2 tablespoons extra virgin olive oil
40 g (1 1/2 oz) butter
2 leeks, trimmed and cut into 5 mm
    (1/4 inch) thick rounds
400 g (14 oz/1 3/4 cups) arborio (risotto) rice
2 granny smith apples, halved lengthways,
    cored and thinly sliced
250 ml (9 fl oz/1 cup) dry white wine
200 g (7 oz) taleggio cheese, chopped
3–4 sage leaves, finely chopped, plus extra
    to garnish

Heat the stock in a saucepan over medium heat and keep at a gentle simmer.

Heat the oil and butter in a large saucepan, add the leek and cook over medium–low heat for 4–5 minutes, or until softened. Add the rice and apples and cook, stirring, for 2–3 minutes, or until the rice is well coated and heated through. Add the wine and cook, stirring, until the wine is absorbed.

Add the simmering stock to the rice mixture, 125 ml (4 fl oz/1/2 cup) at a time, stirring constantly over low heat until all the stock is absorbed. Continue adding the stock, 125 ml (4 fl oz/1/2 cup) at a time, stirring constantly, and waiting until the stock is absorbed before adding more. Cook until the rice is creamy and tender.

Remove from the heat, stir in the taleggio and chopped sage and season to taste with sea salt and freshly ground black pepper. Divide among warmed bowls, decorate with sage leaves and serve immediately.

Apple cinnamon muffins

MAKES 12

310 g (11 oz/2 1/2 cups) self-raising flour
2 teaspoons ground cinnamon
125 g (4 1/2 oz/2/3 cup) soft brown sugar
350 ml (12 fl oz) milk
2 eggs
1 teaspoon natural vanilla extract
150 g (5 1/2 oz) unsalted butter, melted
    and cooled
400 g (14 oz) puréed cooked apples or
    ready-made apple purée
60 g (2 1/4 oz/1/2 cup) walnuts, finely
    chopped

Preheat the oven to 200°C (400°F/Gas 6). Lightly grease a 12-hole standard muffin tin or line the muffin holes with paper cases.

Sift the flour and cinnamon into a bowl and add the sugar. Make a well in the centre. Whisk together the milk, eggs and vanilla and pour into the well in the flour. Add the cooled melted butter.

Fold the mixture gently with a metal spoon until just combined. Add the apple and stir it through the mixture. Do not overmix — the mixture will still be slightly lumpy.

Fill each muffin hole with the mixture (the holes will be quite full, but don't worry because these muffins don't rise as much as some) and sprinkle with the walnuts. Bake for 20–25 minutes, or until golden. Leave in the tin for 5 minutes, then turn out onto a wire rack to cool.

Apple tarte tatin

SERVES 6

100 g (3 1/2 oz) unsalted butter, chopped
185 g (6 1/2 oz/heaped 3/4 cup) sugar
6 large pink lady, fuji or golden delicious
　　apples, peeled, cored and cut into
　　quarters
1 sheet ready-made butter puff pastry
thick (double/heavy) cream or ice cream,
　　to serve

Melt the butter in a frying pan over medium heat. Add the sugar and stir for 4–5 minutes, or until the sugar starts to caramelise. Continue to cook, stirring, until the caramel turns golden brown.

Add the apple quarters to the pan and cook them in two batches over low heat for 20–25 minutes, or until the apples begin to turn golden brown underneath. Carefully turn them over and cook the other side until evenly coloured. Cook off any liquid that comes out of the apples by increasing the heat — the caramel should be sticky rather than runny.

Meanwhile, preheat the oven to 220°C (425°F/Gas 7). Lightly grease a 23 cm (9 inch) shallow cake tin (see note).

Using tongs, arrange the hot apples in the prepared tin, in slightly overlapping circles. Pour the caramel over the top.

Place the pastry sheet over the apples, tucking it down firmly around the edge, using the end of a spoon. Bake for 30–35 minutes, or until the pastry is golden and puffed.

Remove from the oven and leave to cool in the tin for 15 minutes, before inverting onto a serving plate. Serve warm or cold with thick cream or ice cream.

note You could also bake the tarte tatin in a 23 cm (9 inch) ovenproof cast-iron frying pan with an ovenproof handle, as we have done — in which case there is no need to use a cake tin. After the apples have been cooked, arrange them in the frying pan, place the pastry on top and transfer the pan to the oven to bake the pastry.

Apples go well with cider, brandy, cinnamon, nutmeg, cheese, maple syrup, caramel, golden syrup, raisins, blackberries, pears, lemon, orange, chicken, pork, rhubarb, walnuts, almonds, vanilla beans and cream.

The earliest records of **apple** cultivation go back as far as 8000 BC. Apples are mentioned in Homer's *Odyssey*, and Pliny the Elder recorded 20 apple varieties in his tome *Naturalis Historia*. In 1655, a falling apple inspired Sir Isaac Newton to discover the law of gravity, while the familiar phrase 'an apple a day keeps the doctor away' has been repeated to children ever since first stated in a speech in 1904 by the fruit specialist, Professor J.T. Stinson.

Apple and spice teacake

SERVES 8

1 lemon
2 granny smith apples, about 300 g
    (10 1/2 oz) in total
180 g (6 oz) unsalted butter, softened
95 g (3 1/4 oz/1/2 cup) soft brown sugar
3 eggs
125 g (4 1/2 oz/1 cup) self-raising flour
75 g (2 1/2 oz/1/2 cup) wholemeal
    (whole-wheat) flour
1/2 teaspoon ground cinnamon
125 ml (4 fl oz/1/2 cup) milk

topping
1/2 teaspoon mixed spice
1 tablespoon soft brown sugar
25 g (1 oz/1/4 cup) flaked almonds

Preheat the oven to 180°C (350°F/Gas 4). Grease a 20 cm (8 inch) spring-form cake tin and line the base with baking paper.

Grate the zest from the lemon, then juice the lemon into a bowl. Cut the apples in half, then cut out the cores and thinly slice the flesh. Toss the apple slices in the lemon juice to stop them browning. Set aside.

Using electric beaters, cream the butter and sugar until light and fluffy, then beat in the lemon zest. Add the eggs one at a time, beating well after each addition.

Sift the flours and cinnamon into a bowl. Using a large metal spoon, gently fold the flour mixture into the butter mixture, alternating with the milk, until just combined and almost smooth.

Spoon half the batter into the prepared tin, then neatly arrange half the apple slices over the top. Spoon the remaining batter over the apples, then press the remaining apple slices around the top. Combine all the topping ingredients and sprinkle over the cake.

Bake for 1 hour, or until a skewer inserted into the centre of the cake comes out clean. Remove from the oven and leave to cool in the tin for 15 minutes, then turn out onto a wire rack to cool completely.

Store the teacake for up to 2 days in a cool place in an airtight container.

Caramelised apple mousse

SERVES 4

50 g (1¾ oz) unsalted butter
3 tablespoons caster (superfine) sugar
170 ml (5½ fl oz/⅔ cup) whipping cream
500 g (1 lb 2 oz) green apples, peeled,
    cored and cut into thin wedges
2 eggs, separated

Put the butter and sugar in a heavy-based frying pan and stir over low heat until the sugar has dissolved. Increase the heat to medium and cook, stirring, until the mixture turns deep golden. Add 2 tablespoons of the cream and stir until smooth.

Add the apple wedges and cook over medium heat, stirring frequently, for 10–15 minutes, or until the apples are tender and the caramel is very reduced and sticky. Remove eight apple wedges and set aside as a garnish.

Transfer the remaining apples and caramel to a food processor and blend until smooth. Tip into a large bowl, then stir in the egg yolks and leave to cool.

Using electric beaters, whisk the egg whites in a clean, dry bowl until soft peaks form, then gently fold the egg white into the cooled apple mixture.

Whip the remaining cream until firm peaks form, then fold into the apple mixture. Pour into a 750 ml (26 fl oz/3 cup) serving bowl or four 185 ml (6 fl oz/¾ cup) individual ramekins or bowls. Refrigerate for 3 hours, or until firm.

Serve the apple mousse garnished with the reserved apple wedges.

Apple and passionfruit crumble

SERVES 4–6

4 passionfruit
4 green apples
135 g (4¾ oz/⅔ cup) caster (superfine)
    sugar
60 g (2¼ oz/1 cup) shredded coconut
90 g (3¼ oz/¾ cup) plain (all-purpose)
    flour
80 g (2¾ oz) unsalted butter, chopped
thick (double/heavy) cream or ice cream,
    to serve

Preheat the oven to 180°C (350°F/Gas 4). Grease a 1 litre (35 fl oz/4 cup) baking dish.

Push the passionfruit pulp through a sieve, discarding the pulp, and place the juice in a bowl. Peel, core and thinly slice the apples and add to the passionfruit juice, along with 50 g (1¾ oz/¼ cup) of the sugar. Mix well, then transfer the mixture to the baking dish.

Combine the remaining sugar, the coconut, flour and butter in a bowl. Use your fingertips to rub the butter into the coconut and flour until the mixture resembles coarse crumbs. Pile evenly over the apple mixture.

Bake the crumble for 25–30 minutes, or until the topping is crisp and golden. Serve warm with cream or ice cream.

Spiced baked apples

SERVES 4

melted butter, for brushing
4 green apples
3 tablespoons raw (demerara) sugar
3 tablespoons chopped dried figs
3 tablespoons chopped dried apricots
3 tablespoons slivered almonds
1 tablespoon apricot jam
1/4 teaspoon ground cardamom
1/4 teaspoon ground cinnamon
30 g (1 oz) unsalted butter, chopped
whipped cream or ice cream, to serve
    (optional)

Preheat the oven to 180°C (350°F/Gas 4).
Brush a deep baking dish with melted butter.

Peel the apples and remove the cores.
Sprinkle the sugar over a piece of baking
paper and gently roll each apple in the sugar.
In a bowl, mix together the figs, apricots,
almonds, jam and spices.

Fill each apple with some of the fruit mixture.
Place the apples in the baking dish and dot
with pieces of butter.

Bake for 35–40 minutes, or until the apples
are tender. Serve warm with whipped cream
or ice cream, if desired.

note Spiced baked apples are best prepared
and baked just before serving.

Layered potato and apple bake

SERVES 6

2 large potatoes
3 green apples
a squeeze of lemon juice
1 onion
60 g (2 1/4 oz/1/2 cup) finely grated cheddar
    cheese
250 ml (9 fl oz/1 cup) cream
1/4 teaspoon ground nutmeg

Preheat the oven to 180°C (350°F/Gas 4).
Grease a large, shallow baking dish.

Peel the potatoes and cut into thin slices.
Peel, halve and core the apples, then cut into
thin slices. To prevent the potatoes and
apples browning before assembling the dish,
put them in a bowl of cold water with a
squeeze of lemon juice. Drain and pat dry
with paper towels before using. Slice the
peeled onion into very thin rings.

Layer the potatoes, apples and onion in
the prepared dish, finishing with a layer of
potatoes. Sprinkle evenly with cheese, then
pour over the cream. Sprinkle with nutmeg
and freshly ground black pepper, then bake
for 45 minutes, or until golden brown.
Remove from the oven and set aside for
5 minutes before serving. Serve as a side
dish with roast chicken or pork.

Roast pork fillet with apple and mustard sauce

SERVES 4

750 g (1 lb 10 oz) pork fillet
30 g (1 oz) butter
1 tablespoon oil
1 garlic clove, crushed
1/2 teaspoon grated ginger
1 tablespoon seeded mustard
60 ml (2 fl oz/1/4 cup) apple sauce
   (ready-made or see recipe, page 51)
2 tablespoons chicken stock
125 ml (4 fl oz/1/2 cup) cream
1 teaspoon cornflour (cornstarch)

glazed apples
50 g (1 3/4 oz) butter
2 tablespoons soft brown sugar
2 apples, sliced

Preheat the oven to 180°C (350°F/Gas 4).
Trim the pork of fat or sinew. Tie the pork
with kitchen string at intervals so the pork
keeps its shape.

Heat the butter and oil in a frying pan over
medium heat and cook the pork until lightly
browned all over. Lift out the pork and put it
on a rack in a roasting tin. (Leave the cooking
oil in the frying pan.) Add 1/2 cupful of water

to the tin, transfer to the oven and roast for
15–20 minutes. Set aside for 10 minutes
before carving.

Meanwhile, to make the sauce, reheat the oil
in the frying pan, add the garlic and ginger
and cook, stirring, for 1 minute. Stir in the
mustard, apple sauce and stock. Slowly stir
in the combined cream and cornflour and
stir until the sauce boils and thickens.

To make the glazed apples, melt the butter
in a clean frying pan and add the sugar. Stir
until the sugar dissolves. Add the apple slices
and pan-fry, turning occasionally, until the
apples are glazed and lightly browned.

Pour the apple and mustard sauce over the
carved pork and serve with the glazed apples.

Apple and pear sorbet

SERVES 4–6

4 large green apples, peeled, cored and
    chopped
4 pears, peeled, cored and chopped
1 long thick strip of lemon zest
1 cinnamon stick
3 tablespoons lemon juice
4 tablespoons caster (superfine) sugar
2 tablespoons Calvados or Poire William
    liqueur (optional)

Put the apples and pears in a large saucepan
with the strip of lemon zest, cinnamon stick
and enough water to just cover the fruit.
Bring to a simmer, then cover and cook over
low–medium heat for 6–8 minutes, or until
the fruit is tender. Strain the fruit, reserving
4 tablespoons of the cooking liquid, and
discard the lemon zest and cinnamon stick.

Transfer the fruit to a food processor, add the
lemon juice and blend until smooth.

Put the sugar and reserved cooking liquid
in a saucepan, bring to the boil and simmer
for 1 minute. Stir in the fruit purée and the
liqueur, if using.

Pour the fruit purée into a shallow metal tray
and freeze for 2 hours, or until the mixture is
frozen around the edges. Remove from the
fridge and transfer to a food processor and
blend until just smooth, or transfer to a bowl
and beat with a wooden spoon until smooth.

Return to the tray and freeze for a further
2 hours, then process or beat again. Repeat
this process two more times.

Transfer the sorbet to an airtight container,
cover the surface with a piece of baking
paper, then seal with a lid. Freeze until firm.
Serve in small glasses or bowls.

Apple and pear sorbet can be frozen for up
to 3 days.

note You can pour an extra nip of Calvados
over the sorbet to serve, if desired.

Serve slices of crisp **apple** with a cheese platter or add slices
to a winter salad of shaved cucumber, torn witlof and dill, and
serve with poached salmon or trout. Transform ordinary mashed
potato by adding some puréed apple, and serve with sausages.

pear

With their juicy, sweet, aromatic flesh, pears are one of the most widely eaten fruit, after apples. Like many fruit, pears are suited to both sweet and savoury dishes, both cooked and uncooked. They can be poached whole or halved, roasted, sautéed, stewed or simply sliced and used raw. It can be tricky to know just when a pear is perfectly ripe, but when they are, a sweet, juicy pear is hard to resist.

Varieties

Most of the pears eaten today are the results of crosses developed during the seventeenth and eighteenth centuries in Europe and America, as growers tried to develop a variety that was free of the tiny, hard grains within its cells that made pears gritty.

Packham's triumph Also called packham, this popular variety was developed in Australia in 1896. This large pear changes colour from green to pale yellow when ripe and has white, juicy flesh. Eat out of hand or use for cooking, but only when still on the firm side.

Williams Also known as bartlett, this pear is green when unripe but matures to a light yellow, although some varieties are red and variously called red bartlett, red williams or red sensation. These highly aromatic pears have a juicy, buttery flesh. They ripen quickly off the tree and will soften and sweeten at room temperature over 3 days. This all-purpose pear is a good eating pear but can also be poached, baked and used in fruit salads or green salads.

Beurre bosc This elegant pear, with its long, tapering neck, has greenish to brown skin and creamy, full-flavoured flesh. This pear will ripen at room temperature in 3–8 days but it is a harder variety and will not become as soft as other types. This makes it an excellent choice for poaching or roasting for either sweet or savoury dishes.

Comice Generally regarded as one of the finest, this pinkish brown pear is exceptionally juicy and has an excellent smooth texture, rich aromas and intense pear flavour. It bruises very easily, and is not always easy to find. Serve raw with cheese.

Winter nelis This small squat pear has rusted yellow-green skin and is medium to small in size. This variety has a sweet, slightly spicy flesh and is good for cooking or eating raw, although it does have a tough skin.

Corella A small pear with pretty green skin, tinged with a pink blush, this pear has crisp, juicy white flesh. It is unusual in that it may be eaten when hard or soft. These pears make a delicious accompaniment to a cheese platter.

Nashi Also known as the 'pear apple' or 'sand pear', the latter on account of the slight grittiness of its flesh, this pear comes from China, Korea and Japan (*nashi* is the Japanese word for 'pear'). This variety has extremely crisp, juicy, non-acidic sweet flesh that is very mild in flavour.

Buying and storing

- The peak season for pears is from autumn to the end of winter.

- Pears do not ripen well on the tree so are picked when still hard, then transferred to cool storage to cure for a while. They are then brought to room temperature to complete ripening. During ripening, the starches are converted to sugars, and the pear, unusually, ripens from the inside out. Pears can pass through their period of perfect ripeness in a matter of hours, and spoil fairly quickly.

- When allowed to fully tree-ripen, pears are fit to eat for a few days only, after which their flesh turns dry and mealy.

- To tell if a pear is ripe, it should give slightly when pressed with your thumb at the base of the neck; some varieties will also smell a little fragrant. Unlike other pear varieties, nashi pears are picked when ready to eat.

- Buy pears that are unblemished and firm, then ripen them at room temperature — this could take anywhere from 3 to 10 days, depending on the variety.

- Store unripe pears in the fridge for several weeks but make sure there is air circulating around them (don't seal them in plastic) or they may rot. Ideally, store pears in a single layer, as they bruise easily. Nashi pears will keep in the refrigerator for up to 2 weeks.

Preparation

Some pears have tough skin and this is best peeled off. Slice pears just before eating or sprinkle lightly with lemon juice to stop the flesh oxidising.

If poaching or adding to compotes, choose pears that are slightly underripe.

Pear and raspberry crumble

SERVES 4

1.5 kg (3 lb 5 oz) firm ripe pears
    (about 6 large pears)
2 tablespoons caster (superfine) sugar
3 star anise
125 g (4 1/2 oz/1 cup) raspberries
125 g (4 1/2 oz/1 cup) plain (all-purpose)
    flour
95 g (3 1/2 oz/1/2 cup) soft brown sugar
100 g (3 1/2 oz) unsalted butter, chopped
vanilla ice cream, to serve

Preheat the oven to 190°C (375°F/Gas 5).
Peel, quarter and core the pears, then cut
each piece in half lengthways. Put the pears
in a large saucepan and sprinkle the sugar
over them. Add 1 tablespoon water and the
star anise. Cover and bring to the boil, then
cover the pan and cook over medium–low
heat for 10 minutes, stirring occasionally, until
the fruit is tender but still holds its shape.

Drain the pears and discard the star anise.
Transfer to a 1.5 litre (52 fl oz/6 cup) baking
dish. Scatter the raspberries over the pears.

Combine the flour, brown sugar and butter in
a bowl. Using your fingertips, lightly rub in the
butter until the mixture resembles coarse
breadcrumbs. Sprinkle over the fruit, then
bake for 20–25 minutes, or until golden
brown. Set aside for 5 minutes, then serve
with vanilla ice cream.

Pears poached in red wine

SERVES 6

1 tablespoon arrowroot
750 ml (26 fl oz/1 bottle) red wine
110 g (3 3/4 oz/1/2 cup) sugar
1 cinnamon stick
6 cloves
1 small orange, zest removed in strips
1 small lemon, zest removed in strips
6 large firm pears
cream or crème fraîche, to serve

Combine the arrowroot with 2 tablespoons
of the wine in a small bowl and stir to form
a smooth paste. Heat the remaining wine in
a large saucepan with the sugar, cinnamon
stick, cloves and the strips of orange and
lemon zest. Simmer gently for 2–3 minutes,
or until the sugar has dissolved.

Peel the pears, leaving the stalks intact. Add
the pears to the saucepan, cover and cook
over medium heat for 25 minutes, turning
the pears occasionally. When the pears are
very tender, lift them out with a slotted spoon
and put in a deep serving dish.

Strain the spiced wine, discarding the solids,
then return the wine to the saucepan. Stir
the arrowroot again and add it to the hot
wine. Simmer gently, stirring occasionally,
until thickened. Pour the red wine syrup over
the pears and allow to cool. Serve with cream
or crème fraîche.

Spanish duck with paprika, pears and almonds

SERVES 4

stock
1 tablespoon olive oil
1 small carrot, cut into chunks
1 onion, cut into chunks
2 bay leaves
1 thyme sprig
1 parsley sprig
6 black peppercorns

2 kg (4 lb 8 oz) whole duck, cut into
    8 pieces
1/4 teaspoon ground nutmeg
1/2 teaspoon sweet smoked paprika
a pinch of ground cloves
1 tablespoon olive oil
8 French shallots, peeled
8 baby carrots, trimmed
2 garlic cloves, cut into slivers
4 tablespoons rich cream sherry
1 cinnamon stick
4 firm ripe pears, cut in half and
    cored
60 g (2 1/4 oz/heaped 1/3 cup) whole
    blanched almonds, roasted
2 1/2 tablespoons grated dark bittersweet
    chocolate

Make the stock a day ahead using the wings and neck of the duck. Heat the olive oil in a large saucepan, add the duck wings, neck, carrot and onion and cook over medium heat, stirring occasionally, for 15–20 minutes, or until browned. Add 1.25 litres (44 fl oz/ 5 cups) cold water, the bay leaves, thyme and parsley sprigs and peppercorns. Bring to the boil, then reduce the heat to low, cover and simmer for 2 hours. Strain the stock, discarding the solids, then set aside to cool. Refrigerate overnight. The next day, remove the fat off the surface.

Preheat the oven to 180°C (350°F/Gas 4). In a small bowl, combine the nutmeg, paprika and cloves with a little sea salt and freshly ground black pepper. Dust the duck pieces with the spice mixture. Heat the olive oil in a flameproof casserole dish, then brown the duck pieces in batches for 6–7 minutes over medium–high heat, turning once. Set the duck aside.

Drain off all but 1 teaspoon of fat from the dish. Add the shallots and carrots and sauté over medium heat for 3–4 minutes, or until lightly browned. Add the garlic and cook for a further 2 minutes. Add the sherry and stir well to loosen any bits stuck to the bottom of the dish, then add the duck stock, cinnamon stick and all the duck pieces.

Bring to the boil, then cover the dish with a tight-fitting lid and transfer to the oven. Bake for 1 hour 10 minutes, turning the duck halfway through the cooking time. Add the pears and bake for a further 20 minutes, or until the duck is tender.

Meanwhile, process the almonds in a food processor until finely ground. Tip into a bowl, add the chocolate and stir to combine.

Using a slotted spoon, remove the duck and pears from the stock and transfer to a serving plate with the carrots, shallots and cinnamon stick. Cover and keep warm.

Bring the stock to the boil on the stovetop, then cook over high heat for 7–10 minutes, or until reduced by half. Add 3 tablespoons of the hot liquid to the almond and chocolate mixture, stir well, then whisk into the reduced sauce to thicken. Season to taste, then pour over the duck and serve.

Golden ginger pear cake

SERVES 8

85 g (3 oz/$1/4$ cup) golden syrup or light
    corn syrup
250 g (9 oz/2 cups) self-raising flour
2$1/2$ teaspoons ground ginger
140 g (5 oz/$3/4$ cup) soft brown sugar
125 g (4$1/2$ oz) unsalted butter, melted
125 ml (4 fl oz/$1/2$ cup) buttermilk
3 eggs
2 pears, peeled and halved, cores removed,
    then thinly sliced
85 g (3 oz/$1/4$ cup) golden syrup or light
    corn syrup, extra
25 g (1 oz) unsalted butter, extra

Preheat the oven to 180°C (350°F/Gas 4).
Grease an 18 cm (7 inch) round, deep cake
tin and line the base with baking paper. Pour
half the golden syrup over the base of the tin,
spreading evenly with a warmed metal spoon.

Sift the flour and ginger into a bowl, then stir
in the sugar. In a separate bowl, mix together
the melted butter, buttermilk and eggs, then
add to the flour mixture and stir until smooth.
Stir in the pears.

Spoon the batter into the prepared tin and
bake for 1$1/2$ hours, or until a skewer inserted
into the centre of the cake comes out clean.
Remove from the oven and leave to cool in
the tin for 10 minutes, then turn out onto
a serving plate.

To make a syrup glaze, put the extra golden
syrup and extra butter in a small saucepan
and stir over low heat until the butter has
melted and the mixture is smooth. Spoon
the glaze over the cake and serve warm.
The cake is best eaten the day it is made.

Cinnamon pear sauce

MAKES 750 ML (26 FL OZ/3 CUPS)

3 slightly underripe pears
230 g (8 oz/1 cup) caster (superfine) sugar
juice of $1/2$ lemon
2 cinnamon sticks

Peel, core and chop the pears and put them
in a saucepan with 350 ml (12 fl oz) water.
Add the sugar, lemon juice and cinnamon
sticks. Bring to the boil, then reduce the heat
and simmer for 10 minutes, or until the pears
are soft. Remove the cinnamon sticks.

Purée the pears in a blender until smooth.
Serve the cinnamon pear sauce warm over
ice cream, fruit or puddings.

Pear and walnut salad with blue cheese dressing

SERVES 4

dressing
100 g (3 1/2 oz) creamy blue cheese
3 tablespoons olive oil
1 tablespoon walnut oil
1 tablespoon lemon juice
1 tablespoon cream
2 teaspoons finely chopped sage

100 g (3 1/2 oz/1 cup) walnut halves
4 small firm pears
2 tablespoons lemon juice
2 witlof (chicory/Belgian endive), trimmed
    and leaves separated
100 g (3 1/2 oz/1 cup) shaved
    parmesan cheese

To make the dressing, process the blue cheese in a small food processor until smooth, then add the olive oil, walnut oil and lemon juice, and blend until combined well. With the motor running, slowly add 2 teaspoons warm water. Stir in the cream and sage, and season with sea salt and freshly ground black pepper.

Preheat the grill (broiler) to medium–high. Place the walnuts in a bowl and cover with boiling water. Set aside for 1 minute, then drain well. Spread the walnuts on a baking tray and place under the grill for 3 minutes, until lightly toasted. Roughly chop.

Slice the unpeeled pears widthways to make thin rounds; discard the seeds. As each pear is sliced, brush the slices with a little lemon juice to prevent the pears from browning.

Arrange three pear slices in a circle on a serving plate. Top with a scattering of walnuts, a few witlof leaves, then a few more walnuts and some parmesan cheese. Repeat this layering, finishing with a layer of parmesan cheese and some walnuts. Spoon some dressing over each stack. Serve as a first course, or as an accompaniment to simple meat dishes.

Pears team beautifully with cheese (parmesan or blue cheese, a washed-rind or goat's cheese), walnuts, hazelnuts, almonds and pistachios; with salad leaves like radicchio, watercress, spinach and rocket (arugula); and with spices such as ginger, nutmeg, cardamom, saffron, star anise, cloves and cinnamon. Pears are excellent poached in a red wine syrup, or in port or white dessert wine.

Parmesan pears

SERVES 6

3 firm ripe pears, such as packham or
    beurre bosc
40 g (1 1/2 oz) unsalted butter
6 thin slices pancetta, finely chopped
2 spring onions (scallions), thinly sliced
60 g (2 1/4 oz/3/4 cup) fresh white
    breadcrumbs
4 tablespoons grated parmesan cheese

Preheat the grill (broiler) to medium–high.
Cut the pears in half lengthways and remove
the cores.

Melt the butter in a frying pan. Brush the
pears with a little of the melted butter and
place, cut side up, on a tray and grill (broil)
for 4 minutes, or until the pears start to
brown on top.

Add the pancetta and spring onions to the
remaining butter in the pan. Sauté over
medium heat for 3 minutes, or until the
spring onion is soft but not brown. Stir in the
breadcrumbs and some freshly ground black
pepper to taste.

Spoon the pancetta mixture into the pear
cavities, sprinkle with the parmesan cheese
and grill for 3 minutes, or until the cheese
is golden brown. Serve warm as a starter, or
as an accompaniment to roast chicken.

Pear and ginger cheesecake

SERVES 10

250 g (9 oz) plain sweet biscuits
2 tablespoons ground ginger
100 g (3 1/2 oz) unsalted butter, melted

filling
3–4 firm ripe pears
230 g (8 oz/1 cup) caster (superfine) sugar
2 tablespoons lemon juice
500 g (1 lb 2 oz) cream cheese, softened
2 eggs
2 tablespoons ground ginger
300 g (10 1/2 oz) sour cream

Lightly grease a 23 cm (9 inch) spring-form
cake tin and line the base with baking paper.

Finely crush the biscuits with the ginger in
a food processor. Add the butter and mix
well. Spoon the crumbs into the tin and
press firmly onto the base and up the side.
Refrigerate for 10 minutes. Preheat the oven
to 150°C (300°F/Gas 2).

To make the filling, peel, core and thinly slice
the pears. Put them in a saucepan with half
the sugar, the lemon juice and 375 ml
(13 fl oz/1 1/2 cups) water. Bring to the boil,
then reduce the heat and simmer until the
pears are tender but not breaking up. Strain
and set aside to cool.

Process the cream cheese and remaining
sugar in a food processor until light and
smooth. Mix in the eggs and ginger. Add the
sour cream and process to combine. Arrange
the pears over the base, pour over the filling
and bake for 1 hour, or until set. Turn off the
oven and leave to cool with the door ajar,
then refrigerate until firm.

pomegranate

These round fruit, the size of a large apple, have thick, dark red skin that encloses hundreds of small edible fleshy seeds, each encased in a juicy red pulp. Pomegranates are also called Chinese apples, and they are used widely in Persian cuisine as a garnish on sweet and savoury dishes or pressed to extract their tart–sweet juice.

Buying and storing

- Pomegranates are available in markets from autumn to winter.

- Choose pomegranates with smooth skin and those that feel heavy for their size — this indicates the presence of a lot of juice. Generally, larger pomegranates have a sweeter, more developed flavour.

- Store at cool room temperature for 3 weeks or, if in good condition, up to 8 weeks in the fridge; the skin becomes tougher and more leathery with time but this serves to protect the fruit's interior.

- Pomegranate seeds and juice can be frozen for up to 6 months.

Preparation

First cut off the crown of the pomegranate, then cut the fruit into quarters. Put in a large bowl of cold water, then carefully bend the skin back to open up the membranes, prising out the seeds — the bitter white membranes will float to the top of the water, and the seeds will sink. Drain off the water to retrieve the seeds, and pick over the seeds to remove any remaining membrane. Alternatively, bend back the quarters and pick out the seeds.

Juicing Take care when juicing pomegranates as this can be a messy business. Avoid getting the juice on your clothes (it is such an effective stain that it is still used as a dye for Persian carpets). To extract the juice, process the seeds briefly in a food processor, then strain off the juice. As a guide, one pomegranate should yield about 180 g (6 oz/1 cup) of seeds and about 125 ml (4 fl oz/½ cup) of juice.

Pomegranate, green olive and walnut salad

SERVES 4

100 g (3½ oz/1 cup) walnut halves
125 ml (4 fl oz/½ cup) olive oil
1½ tablespoons pomegranate syrup
 (see note)
½ teaspoon chilli flakes
350 g (12 oz/2 cups) green olives, pitted
 and halved
90 g (3¼ oz/½ cup) pomegranate seeds
1 large red onion, chopped
1 large handful flat-leaf (Italian) parsley

Soak the walnut halves in boiling water for 3–4 minutes, or until the skins peel off readily. Drain, peel and pat dry.

Preheat the grill (broiler) to medium. Spread the walnuts on a baking tray and place under the grill for 5 minutes until lightly toasted. Cool, then roughly chop.

Combine the olive oil, pomegranate syrup and chilli flakes in a jar and shake well.

Put the walnuts, olives, pomegranate seeds, onion and parsley in a bowl and toss. Just before serving, pour the dressing over, season with sea salt and freshly ground black pepper, and combine well.

note Pomegranate syrup is available from specialist Middle Eastern food stores and good delicatessens.

Duck breasts with walnut and pomegranate sauce

SERVES 4

4 large duck breasts
1 onion, finely chopped
250 ml (9 fl oz/1 cup) fresh pomegranate
 juice (see preparation, page 72)
2 tablespoons lemon juice
2 tablespoons soft brown sugar
1 teaspoon ground cinnamon
185 g (6½ oz/1½ cups) chopped walnuts
pomegranate seeds, to garnish

Preheat the oven to 180°C (350°F/Gas 4). Using a large knife, score each duck breast two or three times through the skin, taking care not to cut into the flesh.

Place a non-stick frying pan over high heat. Add two of the duck breasts, skin side down, and cook for 6 minutes, or until the skin is crisp and most of the fat has rendered out. Remove from the pan and repeat with the remaining duck breasts. Place in a single layer in a baking dish, skin side up.

Drain all but 1 tablespoon of fat from the pan. Add the onion and sauté over medium–high heat for 5–6 minutes, or until golden. Add the pomegranate juice, lemon juice, sugar, cinnamon and most of the walnuts. Cook for 1 minute, then pour the mixture over the duck breasts. Transfer to the oven and bake for 15 minutes. Remove the duck to a warmed plate, cover loosely with foil and leave to rest in a warm place for 5 minutes.

Skim any excess fat from the sauce. Carve the duck breasts and spoon the sauce over. Garnish with the remaining walnuts and the pomegranate seeds.

quince

The quince is an unpromising looking fruit: rock-hard, thick-skinned and covered with a soft brown or grey down. Yet these fragrant relatives of apples were held sacred by the ancient Greeks as the fruit of Aphrodite, goddess of love. They require long patient cooking, which renders their flesh meltingly soft and transforms it to a glorious rosy colour, and only then are their sweet perfume and flavour fully released. Quinces are suited to poaching, baking, stewing, preserving in syrup, or use them to make jam or sweet quince paste.

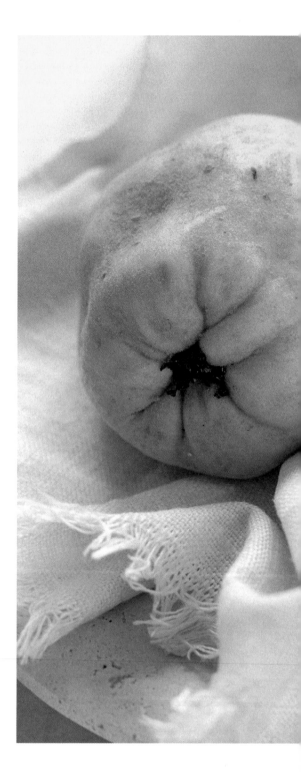

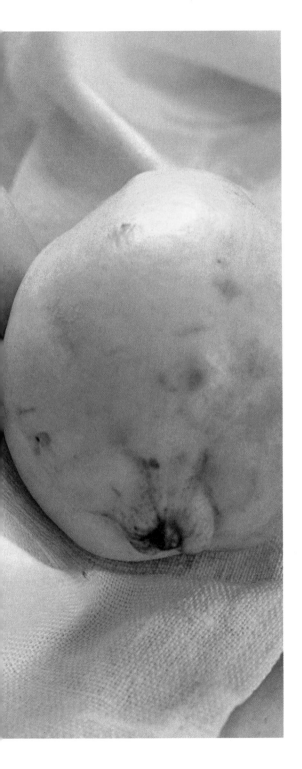

Buying and storing

- Quinces are available in markets from late autumn to winter.

- The two most common varieties are the pineapple quince (an early-ripening variety with large yellow fruit) and smyrna (a smaller quince with a very pronounced flavour and which doesn't break up even when cooked for a very long time). Ask your local grower what variety they have on offer.

- Choose the smoother, larger varieties as these are easier to prepare and less wasteful. Buy fruit with bright yellow or gold skin, with no signs of green or discolouration.

- Riper fruit tends to have less fuzz on its skin, although the amount of fuzz present can also be a feature of the variety.

- Quinces will store at cool room temperature for 10–14 days, and for up to 3 weeks in the fridge (seal the fruit in a plastic bag to prevent their aroma permeating everything in the fridge).

Preparation

Before cooking, wash well to remove any fuzz. If making jam (quinces are high in pectin, so are ideal for this) don't bother to peel or core them as the flavour will be better and the flotsam gets strained out at the end anyway. Otherwise, peel and core your quinces and remove the seeds. They go brown instantly, so rub the cut surfaces with lemon juice as you cut them or put the pieces in water with a squeeze of lemon juice.

Quinces are an ancient fruit and one theory suggests that it was actually a quince or pomegranate, and not the apple, that tempted Eve in the Garden of Eden. The quince originated around the Black and Caspian Seas. It made its way westward, and became popular throughout Mediterranean Europe, Northern Africa and Portugal. Called *marmelos* by the Portuguese and *membrillo* by the Spanish, the quince is the source of the English word 'marmalade' — the original marmalade was made using quince.

Quince paste

MAKES ABOUT 1 KG (2 LB 4 OZ)

3 large quinces
800 g (1 lb 12 oz/3²/₃ cups) sugar, approximately

Wash the quinces, then place them in a saucepan and add enough water to cover. Bring to the boil, then reduce the heat and simmer for 30 minutes, or until tender. Drain and leave until they are cool enough to handle. Peel and core the quinces, then push them through a sieve, food mill or potato ricer, discarding the solids.

Weigh the quince pulp and place in a heavy-based saucepan. Measure the same weight of sugar as the quince pulp and add to the saucepan. Simmer over low heat, stirring occasionally, for 3¹/₂–4¹/₂ hours, or until very thick, taking care not to let the mixture burn. Remove from the heat and allow to cool a little.

Line a 28 x 18 cm (11 x 7 inch) rectangular cake tin or dish with plastic wrap, then pour the quince mixture into the tin and set aside to cool.

The quince paste can be kept for several months in a tightly sealed container in the fridge. Serve with cheese and bread or crackers, or with game such as pheasant.

Slow-baked quinces in honey

SERVES 8

60 g (2¼ oz) unsalted butter
8 quinces
2 tablespoons honey
125 ml (4 fl oz/½ cup) sweet white dessert
    wine, such as Sauternes
thick (double/heavy) cream or vanilla ice
    cream, to serve

Preheat the oven to 150°C (300°F/Gas 2).
Use half the butter to lightly grease a shallow
ovenproof dish that is large enough to hold
the halved quinces in one layer (they can
overlap slightly).

Peel and halve the quinces. Don't worry
about them discolouring, as they will turn
very dark during cooking. Remove the cores.
Put them, cut side up, in the prepared dish.

Drizzle the honey and wine over the quinces
and dot with the remaining butter. Cover with
foil and bake for 2 hours, then turn the
quinces over and bake for a further 2 hours.
The quinces should be a rich maroon red and
the juices caramelised. Serve hot or warm
with cream or softened vanilla ice cream.

Poached quince on brioche

SERVES 8

2 large quinces
lemon juice, for brushing
350 g (12 oz/1½ cups) caster (superfine)
    sugar
1 vanilla bean
1 cinnamon stick
1 cardamom pod
8 slices brioche
ground cinnamon, to sprinkle
caster (superfine) sugar, to sprinkle

Peel and halve the quinces, them remove the
cores and cut them into quarters. Brush the
flesh with a little lemon juice to prevent them
turning brown.

Put 350 ml (12 fl oz) water, the sugar, vanilla
bean, cinnamon stick and cardamom pod in
a saucepan. Bring to the boil, stirring until the
sugar has dissolved. Add the quinces, cover
and simmer for 2–3 hours, or until they are
very tender. Remove from the pan, then
simmer the cooking liquid until reduced to
a syrup, then strain.

Toast the brioche slices and butter lightly.
Sprinkle the brioche with a little cinnamon
and sugar and top with the poached quinces.
Drizzle some syrup over the top and serve
hot or cold.

Lamb tagine with quince

SERVES 4–6

1.5 kg (3 lb 5 oz) boned lamb shoulder
2 large handfuls coriander (cilantro),
    chopped
2 large onions, diced
1/2 teaspoon ground ginger
1/2 teaspoon cayenne pepper
1/4 teaspoon ground saffron threads
1 teaspoon ground coriander
1 cinnamon stick
500 g (1 lb 2 oz) quinces
40 g (1 1/2 oz) butter
100 g (3 1/2 oz/1/2 cup) dried apricots
1 tablespoon caster (superfine) sugar
coriander (cilantro) leaves, to garnish
couscous or rice, to serve

Cut the lamb into 3 cm (1 1/4 inch) pieces. Put the lamb in a heavy-based flameproof casserole dish. Add the coriander leaves, half the onion, the ginger, cayenne pepper, saffron threads, ground coriander and cinnamon stick. Season with sea salt and freshly ground black pepper.

Cover with cold water and bring to the boil over medium heat. Lower the heat and simmer, partly covered, for 1 1/2 hours, or until the lamb is tender.

Meanwhile, peel and core the quinces and cut them into thick wedges. Melt the butter in a heavy-based frying pan over medium heat and cook the quinces and remaining onion for 15 minutes, or until lightly golden. When the lamb has been cooking for 1 hour, add the quince mixture, dried apricots and sugar.

Taste the sauce and adjust the seasoning if necessary. Transfer to a warm serving dish and garnish with coriander leaves. Serve immediately with couscous or rice.

Quinces complement apples and pears, and these other fruit can be used to extend your supply of quinces — when cooked together, the quinces' flavour overpowers the more neutral ones of apples and pears.

rhubarb

Although it is botanically classified as a vegetable, rhubarb is generally used in cooking as a fruit. However, only the stalks are edible as the leaves contain oxalic acid (the stalks do too but unless eaten in great quantities they won't cause you any harm). This may explain why rhubarb was slow to gain popularity in Europe, as early experimenters consumed the leaves with dire results. It wasn't until the nineteenth century, when strains of the plant were developed that had juicy, tender stalks, that rhubarb became popular, particularly with cooks from England and North America.

Buying and storing

- The first rhubarb stalks to appear in early spring are the most tender. Field-grown rhubarb tends to be juicier, sourer, less tender and darker red than that grown in greenhouses. Some cooks prefer the fuller flavour and thicker stems of field-grown rhubarb, while others prefer the softer texture and gentler flavour of greenhouse rhubarb.

- Look for stalks that are firm and upright, avoiding very thick ones as these will be fibrous. Stalks range in colour from pink and red to green, although generally the red stalks are sweeter.

- Rhubarb is usually sold with its leaves attached. These should be removed as they contain poisonous oxalic acid. Wrap the stalks in plastic wrap and store in the fridge for up to 1 week.

Preparation

Rhubarb is generally cooked, or stewed, with sugar for use in sweet dishes such as fools, jams, compotes, crumbles and pies.

Stewing First slice 1 kg (2 lb 4 oz) rhubarb into 2 cm (¾ inch) pieces. Any tough stalks should be peeled first (be careful as the juice can stain clothing). Put the chopped stalks in a saucepan with 115 g (4 oz/½ cup) caster (superfine) sugar and 2 tablespoons water. Don't add the sugar all at once — add it in small amounts to begin with, then add more to taste as the rhubarb cooks (rhubarb can vary widely in sourness). Cover the saucepan and simmer, stirring occasionally, for 5–8 minutes, or until tender. Serve hot, warm or chilled with some cream, custard, or vanilla or strawberry ice cream to cut the acid edge.

Rhubarb can be flavoured with a little rosewater or cinnamon, sweetened with honey instead of sugar, or cooked with a little orange juice and finely grated orange zest. Rhubarb teams well with oranges in marmalade, and a rhubarb and strawberry combination works well as a pie filling or crumble base. For savoury dishes, rhubarb goes well with meats such as duck and, lightly sweetened and puréed, it makes a wonderful sauce for pork.

Rhubarb and apple upside-down cake

SERVES 6–8

250 g (9 oz/heaped 1 cup) sugar
250 g (9 oz) rhubarb, chopped into 2 cm
   (3/4 inch) pieces
1 small apple, peeled, cored and chopped
2 eggs
40 g (1 1/4 oz/1/3 cup) icing (confectioners')
   sugar
1/2 teaspoon natural vanilla extract
100 g (3 1/2 oz) unsalted butter, melted
   and cooled
125 g (4 1/2 oz/1 cup) self-raising flour

Preheat the oven to 180°C (350°F/Gas 4). Lightly grease a deep 20 cm (8 inch) round cake tin and line the base with baking paper.

Put the sugar in a small saucepan with 4 tablespoons water and heat gently, shaking the pan occasionally, until the sugar has dissolved. Increase the heat and cook until it turns a pale caramel colour — it will turn a deeper colour in the oven. Pour into the prepared tin and then press the rhubarb and apple into the caramel.

Beat the eggs, icing sugar and vanilla extract in a small bowl with electric beaters until the mixture is frothy. Fold in the melted butter. Sift the flour over the top and stir to combine (the mixture will be soft). Spoon gently over the fruit, being careful not to dislodge it.

Transfer to the oven and bake for 45 minutes, or until set on top. Run a knife around the side of the cake and turn out very carefully onto a wire rack to cool. Be sure to do this straight away, otherwise the caramel will cool and stick to the tin. Remove the baking paper. Serve warm with cream as a dessert, or cool and serve as a teacake.

note Fresh plums can be substituted for the apple and rhubarb in this recipe. Halve the plums, remove the stones, then slice them. Press the plum slices into the caramel in a decorative spiral pattern, or randomly. Bake the cake as for the original recipe.

Farmhouse rhubarb pie

SERVES 6

185 g (6$\frac{1}{2}$ oz/1$\frac{1}{2}$ cups) plain (all-purpose)
   flour
2 tablespoons icing (confectioners') sugar
125 g (4$\frac{1}{2}$ oz) cold unsalted butter,
   chopped
1 egg yolk, mixed with 1 tablespoon
   iced water
ground cinnamon and sugar, to sprinkle
icing (confectioners') sugar, to dust

filling
220 g (7$\frac{3}{4}$ oz/1 cup) sugar
750 g (1 lb 10 oz/6 cups) chopped rhubarb
2 large apples, peeled, cored and chopped
2 teaspoons finely grated lemon zest
3 pieces preserved ginger, sliced

Sift the flour, icing sugar and a pinch of salt into a large bowl. Using your fingertips, lightly rub the butter into the flour until the mixture resembles coarse breadcrumbs. Make a well in the centre. Add the egg yolk mixture to the well and mix using a flat-bladed knife until a rough dough forms. Gently gather the dough together, transfer to a lightly floured surface, then press into a round disc. Cover with plastic wrap and refrigerate for 30 minutes, or until firm.

Preheat the oven to 190°C (375°F/Gas 5). Grease a 20 cm (8 inch) pie dish.

Roll the pastry out to a 35 cm (14 inch) circle and ease it into the dish, allowing the excess to hang over the edge. Put the pastry-lined dish in the fridge while you prepare the filling.

To make the filling, put the sugar and 125 ml (4 fl oz/$\frac{1}{2}$ cup) water in a saucepan and cook for 4–5 minutes, until syrupy. Add the rhubarb, apples, lemon zest and ginger. Cover and gently simmer for 5 minutes, or until the rhubarb is cooked but still holds its shape.

Drain off the liquid and allow the rhubarb to cool. Spoon the rhubarb into the pastry shell and sprinkle with the cinnamon and sugar. Fold the overhanging pastry over the filling. Transfer to the oven and bake for 40 minutes, or until golden. Dust the pie with icing sugar before serving.

The use of **rhubarb** as a food crop is only recent. Rhubarb was an important medicine crop in China, and from there it was eventually exported to Europe, where it became incredibly popular. In sixteenth-century France, rhubarb was reputed to be ten times as expensive as cinnamon — in England in the 1650s, it sold for over two and a half times the price of opium!

soft fruit

Buying and storing

- Blackberries are in season from late summer to autumn.

- Buy soft, plump blackberries with no stems attached — this indicates they were picked too early and may be underripe and tasteless. Eat them soon after purchase as they lose their flavour quickly.

- To freeze blackberries, spread them in a single layer on trays lined with baking paper. (Freezing the berries in a single layer first prevents them from clumping if frozen all at once.) When frozen, transfer to an airtight container or freezer bag, pressing all the air out of the bag. Use within 6 months.

blackberry

Wild blackberries grow on prickly rambling bushes, and in some areas they are considered a noxious weed. Blackberries are botanically not berries at all, but are part of the rose (Rosaceae) family. The cultivation of the blackberry has resulted in the elimination of their thorny branches, which makes harvesting much easier.

Wild blackberries are smaller than cultivated berries but are more intensely flavoured. Containing high levels of pectin, slightly underripe blackberries are ideal for making jams, jellies and preserves. While they're great in compotes, tarts and pies, they are perhaps at their best served simply with a dollop of thick cream.

Blackberry and apple jam

MAKES 1.75 LITRES (61 FL OZ/7 CUPS)

750 g (1 lb 10 oz) green apples
    (about 5 apples)
1 kg (2 lb 4 oz/8 cups) fresh blackberries,
    boysenberries or raspberries
1.5 kg (3 lb 5 oz/7 cups) sugar

Peel, core and chop the apples. Put the apple pieces in a large saucepan with the berries and 125 ml (4 fl oz/$\frac{1}{2}$ cup) water. Cook, covered, over medium heat, stirring often, for 30 minutes, or until the fruit have softened.

Meanwhile, warm the sugar slightly by first spreading the sugar in a large baking tin and then heating it in a 120°C (235°F/Gas $\frac{1}{2}$) oven for 10 minutes, stirring occasionally. Put two small plates in the freezer.

Add the warmed sugar to the fruit all at once. Stir over low heat, without boiling, for 5 minutes, or until the sugar has dissolved. Bring the jam to the boil, then boil for 20 minutes, stirring often. Stir across the base of the pan to check that the jam is not sticking or burning. When the jam falls from a wooden spoon in thick sheets without dripping, start testing for setting point.

To do this, remove the pan from the heat. Put a little of the jam onto one of the cold plates and return the plate to the freezer for 30 seconds. When setting point is reached, a skin should form on the surface and the jam should wrinkle when pushed with your finger. If not, continue to reduce the syrup over heat and use the second plate to test for setting point.

Transfer the jam to a heatproof jug and immediately pour into hot sterilised jars (see page 24), and seal. Turn the jars upside down for 2 minutes, then turn back up again and leave to cool. Label and date for storage.

Store in a cool, dark place for 6–12 months. Once opened, the jam will keep in the fridge for 6 weeks.

To make a **blackberry butter** for pancakes, crumpets or scones, simply combine some blackberries, a little icing (confectioners') sugar and some softened unsalted butter in a food processor until smooth.

Blackberries are called brambles in the United Kingdom. According to local folklore, blackberries should not be picked after 29 September (Michaelmas or the feast of St Michael), when it is said that the devil claims them for his own evil uses.

Bramble pie

SERVES 4–6

125 g (4½ oz/1 cup) self-raising flour
125 g (4½ oz/1 cup) plain (all-purpose) flour
2 tablespoons caster (superfine) sugar
125 g (4½ oz) cold unsalted butter, chopped
1 egg, lightly beaten
3–4 tablespoons milk

filling
2 tablespoons cornflour (cornstarch)
2–4 tablespoons caster (superfine) sugar, to taste
1 teaspoon finely grated orange zest
1 tablespoon orange juice
600 g (1 lb 5 oz) brambles (see note)

glaze
1 egg yolk, mixed with 1 teaspoon water

Sift the flours into a large bowl and add the sugar. Using your fingertips, lightly rub in the butter until the mixture resembles fine breadcrumbs. Make a well in the centre, then add the egg and most of the milk to the well. Mix using a flat-bladed knife until a rough dough forms, adding a little more milk if necessary. Turn out onto a lightly floured work surface, then gently press together into a ball. Form into a flat disc, cover with plastic wrap and refrigerate for 30 minutes.

Meanwhile, preheat the oven to 180°C (350°F/Gas 4).

To make the filling, combine the cornflour, sugar, orange zest and orange juice in a saucepan. Add half the berries and stir over low heat for 5 minutes, or until the mixture boils and thickens. Leave to cool, then stir in the remaining berries. Pour into a 750 ml (26 fl oz/3 cup) pie dish.

Cut the chilled dough in half. Roll out one portion on a lightly floured work surface until large enough to cover the top of the dish, trimming away the excess. Roll out the other half and, using heart-shaped pastry cutters of various sizes, cut out some hearts to decorate the pie. Brush the pie with the glaze and transfer to the oven. Bake for 35 minutes, or until golden brown. Serve hot or warm.

note Brambles include any creeping stem berries, such as boysenberries, blackberries, loganberries and youngberries. You can use just one variety or a combination.

Currants are relatives of the gooseberry family. Redcurrants are popular in Northern European cuisine and are commonly cooked in jams and sauces, such as the British cumberland sauce, and are the traditional ingredient in summer pudding. Redcurrants and their many hybrids, including the white currant, have thinner skins and sweeter flesh than blackcurrants and can be eaten raw.

Venison with blackberry sauce

SERVES 4

60 g (2 1/4 oz) clarified butter (see note)
12 baby onions, peeled with roots left intact
150 g (5 1/2 oz/1 cup) blackberries or
    blackcurrants
3 tablespoons redcurrant jelly
16 x 50 g (1 3/4 oz) venison medallions
3 tablespoons red wine
400 ml (14 fl oz) beef stock
2 teaspoons butter, softened
2 teaspoons plain (all-purpose) flour

Melt half the butter in a saucepan, then add the onions. Cover and cook over low heat for 20–25 minutes, stirring occasionally, until the onions are golden and soft. Set aside.

Put the berries in a separate saucepan with the redcurrant jelly and 3 tablespoons water. Stir to combine, then boil for 5 minutes, or until the berries have softened and the liquid has reduced and is syrupy. Set aside.

Season the venison with sea salt and freshly ground black pepper. Heat the remaining butter in a frying pan and cook the venison

in batches over high heat for 1–2 minutes, turning once. Transfer the venison to a plate, cover loosely with foil and keep warm in a 120°C (235°F/Gas 1/2) oven.

Add the wine to the frying pan and boil for 30 seconds, then add the stock and boil until reduced by half. Mix together the softened butter and flour to make a smooth paste, then whisk it into the stock, stirring constantly. Bring the mixture to the boil and cook for 2 minutes, or until slightly thickened.

Strain the syrup from the berries into the frying pan and stir well. Season with sea salt and freshly ground black pepper. Serve the venison and onions with the sauce, using the drained berries as a garnish.

note To make clarified butter, melt 250 g (9 oz) unsalted butter in a pan over low heat. Bring to a simmer and cook to evaporate off the water. Skim off the white foam from the surface, then pour off the clarified golden butter, leaving the white sediment behind in the pan. Store in the fridge for 3–4 weeks.

Summer pudding

SERVES 4-6

150 g (5 1/2 oz/1 1/4 cups) blackcurrants
150 g (5 1/2 oz/1 1/4 cups) redcurrants
150 g (5 1/2 oz/1 1/4 cups) raspberries
150 g (5 1/2 oz/1 1/4 cups) blackberries
200 g (7 oz/1 1/3 cups) strawberries,
    hulled and halved
caster (superfine) sugar, to taste
6-8 slices good-quality day-old sliced
    white bread, crusts removed
whipped cream, to serve

Put all the berries, except the strawberries, in a large saucepan with 125 ml (4 fl oz/1/2 cup) water and heat gently until the berries begin to collapse. Add the strawberries and turn off the heat. Add sugar to taste (the amount you need will depend on how ripe and sweet the berries are). Set aside to cool.

Line a 1 litre (35 fl oz/4 cup) pudding basin (mould) with bread, cutting a large circle out of one slice for the base and slicing the rest into strips to line the side of the basin.

Drain a little juice off the fruit mixture. Dip one side of each piece of bread into the juice before fitting it, juice side down, into the basin, leaving no gaps. Do not squeeze or flatten the bread or it will not absorb the juices well.

Fill the centre of the mould with the berries, reserving any leftovers, and add a little juice. Cover the top with a layer of dipped bread, juice side up, and cover with plastic wrap. Put a plate which fits tightly inside the basin onto the plastic wrap to weigh it down. Refrigerate overnight. Carefully turn out the pudding and serve with any reserved berry mixture and whipped cream.

Blackcurrants are shiny, tiny, purple-black berries. They have an astringent, somewhat musky sourness, and are one of the few fruit that need to be cooked with a little sugar to temper their tartness. Blackcurrants are used in jellies, preserves and sauces, and in the French liqueur crème de cassis, the essential ingredient in the champagne cocktail kir royale.

blueberry

The very best blueberry recipes — blueberry-studded muffins, cheesecakes and homely pies — come from North America, where the blueberry is native and was a key source of nutrition for the North American Indian population.

Buying and storing

- The peak season for blueberries is from late spring to summer.

- Choose plump, firm, uniformly sized blueberries coated with a dusty silver-white bloom — this indicates freshness and is their natural protection against the sun.

- Check there are no squashed or mouldy berries lurking at the bottom of the container.

- If not using straightaway, transfer unwashed blueberries to a dish lined with paper towel, cover with plastic wrap and refrigerate for up to 2 days.

- Freeze blueberries for up to 6 months. Don't wash them before freezing as this tends to toughen their skin.

Preparation

Simplicity itself. Wash blueberries just before eating or cooking, then drain on paper towels. If adding them to cake and muffin batters, do it at the last moment to prevent their juices from streaking the mixture. In pancakes, to seal in their juice and prevent overcooking them, scatter them over half-cooked batter in the pan before turning.

For baking or making jams, pancakes and salads, blueberries work well with the flavours of lemon (which can turn them red), cinnamon, cloves, pecans, almonds, peaches, yoghurt and fromage frais.

Blueberry cheesecake

SERVES 8–10

125 g (4$\frac{1}{2}$ oz) unsalted butter
100 g (3$\frac{1}{2}$ oz/1 cup) rolled (porridge) oats
100 g (3$\frac{1}{2}$ oz) wheatmeal biscuits, finely
  crushed
2 tablespoons soft brown sugar
250 g (9 oz/1$\frac{2}{3}$ cups) fresh blueberries
240 g (8$\frac{1}{2}$ oz/$\frac{3}{4}$ cup) blackberry jam
3 tablespoons cherry brandy

filling
375 g (13 oz/1$\frac{1}{2}$ cups) cream cheese,
  at room temperature
100 g (3$\frac{1}{2}$ oz/heaped $\frac{1}{3}$ cup) ricotta
  cheese
4 tablespoons caster (superfine) sugar
125 g (4$\frac{1}{2}$ oz/$\frac{1}{2}$ cup) sour cream
2 eggs
1 tablespoon finely grated orange zest
1 tablespoon plain (all-purpose) flour

Grease a deep, 20 cm (8 inch) round
spring-form cake tin and line the base with
baking paper.

Melt the butter in a saucepan, add the oats
and biscuit crumbs and mix well. Stir in the
brown sugar.

Press half the biscuit mixture firmly over the
base of the cake tin, then gradually press the
remainder around the side of the tin, using
a glass to firm it into place, and pressing it
about three-quarters of the way up to the
edge. Refrigerate the crust for 10–15 minutes,
or until firm.

Meanwhile, preheat the oven to 180°C
(350°F/Gas 4).

To make the filling, put the cream cheese,
ricotta, sugar and sour cream in a bowl and
beat using electric beaters until smooth. Beat
in the eggs, orange zest and flour.

Set the cake tin on a baking tray, then pour
the filling into the crust. Transfer the cake tin
on the baking tray to the oven and bake for
40–45 minutes, or until the filling is just set.
Remove from the oven and leave in the tin
to cool.

Arrange the blueberries over the cooled
cheesecake. Put the jam and cherry brandy
in a small saucepan and gently heat until the
jam has melted. Simmer for 1–2 minutes,
then remove from the heat and push the
mixture through a sieve into a bowl. Allow to
cool slightly, then carefully brush the mixture
over the blueberries.

Refrigerate the cheesecake for several hours
or overnight before serving. The cheesecake
will store for up to 2 days in the fridge.

Blueberry pancake stack

SERVES 4

pancakes
185 g (6 1/2 oz/1 1/2 cups) self-raising flour
1 teaspoon baking powder
2 tablespoons caster (superfine) sugar
2 eggs
250 ml (9 fl oz/1 cup) milk
60 g (2 1/4 oz) unsalted butter, melted,
    plus extra for brushing
155 g (5 1/2 oz/1 cup) fresh blueberries

100 g (3 1/2 oz) unsalted butter, softened
maple syrup, to serve

To make the pancakes, sift the flour, baking powder, sugar and a pinch of salt into a large bowl and make a well in the centre. Whisk the eggs, milk and melted butter together in a jug, then pour into the well in the flour mixture all at once, whisking to form a smooth batter. Cover with plastic wrap and leave to stand for 20 minutes.

Meanwhile, preheat the oven to 120°C (235°F/Gas 1/2).

Place a frying pan over low heat and brush lightly with melted butter. Stir the blueberries into the pancake batter. Pour about 60 ml (2 fl oz/1/4 cup) of batter into the pan and swirl gently to make a pancake about 10 cm (4 inches) in diameter. Cook for 1 minute, or until golden underneath, then flip the pancake over and cook for about 10 seconds. Transfer to the oven to keep warm while you cook the remaining pancakes.

Using a wooden spoon or electric beaters, beat the softened butter until light and fluffy. Stack the pancakes on individual serving plates and serve warm or cold, with the whipped butter and maple syrup.

The blueberry pancakes are best eaten the day they are made.

Containing cholesterol-lowering compounds, antioxidants, vitamin C, potassium, folate and dietary fibre, **blueberries** are regarded as one of the so-called 'super foods'. Research suggests that they have anti-ageing properties as well.

Berry trifle

SERVES 8–10

550 g (1 lb 4 oz/1¾ cups) redcurrant jelly
170 ml (5½ fl oz/⅔ cup) orange juice
625 ml (21½ fl oz/2½ cups) whipping
   cream
250 g (9 oz) mascarpone cheese
30 g (1 oz/¼ cup) icing (confectioners')
   sugar
1 teaspoon natural vanilla extract
¼ teaspoon ground cinnamon
250 g (9 oz) savoiardi (lady fingers/sponge
   finger biscuits)
375 ml (13 fl oz/1½ cups) sweet Marsala
200 g (7 oz) fresh raspberries
200 g (7 oz) fresh redcurrants
200 g (7 oz) large fresh strawberries, hulled
   and quartered
200 g (7 oz) fresh blueberries
200 g (7 oz) fresh blackberries (see note)

Melt the redcurrant jelly in a small saucepan over medium heat. Remove from the heat, stir in the orange juice and set aside until the mixture cools to room temperature.

Using electric beaters, beat the cream, mascarpone, icing sugar, vanilla and cinnamon in a bowl until soft peaks form.

Cut each biscuit in half widthways and, working with half the biscuits, dip them in the Marsala and arrange over the base of a 3.25 litre (110 fl oz/13 cup) serving bowl.

Sprinkle a third of the combined berries over the biscuits and drizzle with half of the remaining Marsala and a third of the redcurrant sauce. Spoon half the cream mixture over the sauce. Repeat the layering with the remaining biscuits, again dipping them in the Marsala, a third of the berries and sauce, and the remaining cream. Arrange the remaining berries over the cream.

Reserve the final third of the redcurrant sauce. Cover the trifle with plastic wrap and refrigerate overnight. Before serving, pour the reserved redcurrant sauce over the berries to glaze. (Warm the sauce slightly if it has thickened too much.)

note Any selection of fresh berries, to a total weight of 1 kg (2 lb 4 oz), can be used. Frozen berries are unsuitable for this recipe.

Currants are often sold attached to their stalks. The easiest way to remove them from the stalks is to slide the tines of a fork down either side of the stalk, popping off the berries.

For a simple **blueberry topping** for vanilla ice cream, briefly heat some berries in a pan with sugar and a splash of brandy or balsamic vinegar.

Berries in champagne jelly

SERVES 8

1 litre (35 fl oz/4 cups) champagne
    or sparkling white wine
1½ tablespoons powdered gelatine
220 g (7¾ oz/1 cup) sugar
4 strips of lemon zest
4 strips of orange zest
250 g (9 oz/1⅔ cups) small strawberries,
    hulled and halved
250 g (9 oz/1⅔ cups) blueberries

Pour 500 ml (17 fl oz/2 cups) of the champagne into a bowl and let the bubbles subside. Sprinkle the gelatine evenly over the champagne, then leave to stand for 5 minutes, or until the gelatine has softened.

Pour the remaining champagne into a large saucepan. Add the sugar and strips of orange and lemon zests. Heat gently, stirring constantly for 3 minutes, or until the sugar has dissolved.

Remove the pan from the heat, add the gelatine mixture and stir until dissolved. Set aside to cool, then remove the strips of zest.

Divide the berries among eight small wine glasses or martini glasses and carefully pour the jelly over the top. Refrigerate for 6 hours or overnight, or until the jelly has set.

Remove from the refrigerator 15 minutes before serving.

Spiced blueberry sauce

MAKES 250 ML (9 FL OZ/1 CUP)

300 g (10½ oz/2 cups) fresh or frozen
    blueberries
55 g (2 oz/¼ cup) caster (superfine) sugar
1 cinnamon stick
2 strips of orange zest
1 strip of lemon zest
1 teaspoon lemon juice

Combine the blueberries, sugar, cinnamon stick, strips of orange and lemon zests, lemon juice and 2 tablespoons water in a saucepan over low heat. Cover and cook, stirring occasionally, for 2–3 minutes, or until the sugar has dissolved.

Bring to a simmer and cook for 5 minutes, or until the blueberries are soft and the sauce has thickened slightly. Remove the cinnamon stick and strips of zest. Cool a little before serving. Drizzle over ice cream or yoghurt, or serve with chocolate or sponge cakes.

Orange and blueberry rolls

MAKES 20

250 ml (9 fl oz/1 cup) milk, warmed
4 teaspoons dried yeast
80 g (2¾ oz/⅓ cup) caster (superfine)
   sugar
125 g (4½ oz) unsalted butter, softened
4 tablespoons orange juice
2 eggs, lightly beaten
375 g (13 oz/3 cups) strong flour
icing (confectioners') sugar, for dusting

filling
100 g (3½ oz) unsalted butter, softened
115 g (4 oz/½ cup) caster (superfine) sugar
finely grated zest of 2 oranges
270 g (9½ oz/1¾ cups) fresh blueberries

Pour 100 ml (3½ fl oz) of the warm milk into a small bowl. Sprinkle with the yeast and a pinch of the sugar and leave in a draught-free place for 10 minutes, or until foamy.

Put the remaining warmed milk and sugar in the bowl of an electric mixer along with the butter and 1 teaspoon salt. Using the beater attachment, mix until the butter has just melted. Add the orange juice, eggs and yeast mixture and mix to combine. With the mixer set to the lowest speed, gradually add the flour, 60 g (2¼ oz/½ cup) at a time, mixing until a smooth dough forms.

Place the dough in a large oiled bowl, turning to coat in the oil. Cover with plastic wrap and leave the dough to rise in a draught-free place for 1 hour, or until doubled in size.

To make the filling, cream the butter, sugar and orange zest in a small bowl using electric beaters until pale and fluffy.

Turn the dough out onto a lightly floured work surface and divide in half. Roll each piece into a 25 x 15 cm (10 x 6 inch) rectangle. Spread half the filling mixture over one rectangle, then arrange half the blueberries over the top. Repeat with the remaining dough, filling and blueberries. Starting from the long side, roll up each rectangle to form a cylinder. Using a lightly floured, serrated knife, cut each cylinder into ten even rolls.

Grease two 20 cm (8 inch) round spring-form cake tins. Arrange half the rolls, cut side up, in each tin. Cover with a damp tea towel and set aside to rise in a draught-free place for 45 minutes, or until doubled in size. Meanwhile, preheat the oven to 180°C (350°F/Gas 4).

Bake the rolls for 25–30 minutes, or until they are golden and coming away from the side of the tins. Remove from the oven and leave to cool in the tins for 5 minutes, then turn out onto a wire rack to cool completely. Dust with icing sugar to serve.

Orange and blueberry rolls are best eaten the day they are made.

To make a **boysenberry gratin**, scatter some berries into a small baking dish. Drizzle with crème de cassis, then top with crème fraîche and soft brown sugar. Place under a hot grill (broiler) until bubbling and golden.

boysenberry

A cross between a raspberry, blackberry and a loganberry, these berries are thought to have been developed by an American horticulturalist Rudolph Boysen. From berry compotes and pies to refreshing sorbets and gelatos, these sweet–sour summer berries can be used interchangeably or in combination with any other berry.

Buying and storing

- Boysenberries are in season during summer.
- Buy berries that are uniform in size with no signs of mould or shrivelling.
- Boysenberries are highly perishable and should preferably be eaten the day you buy them. Alternatively, store them in a single layer on paper towel in an airtight container in the fridge for up to 2 days.
- The berries can be frozen for up to 3 months, although they'll only be good for cooking.

Preparation

Don't wash boysenberries before use, as this dilutes their flavour; simply wipe them with a damp cloth.

Boysenberries have a sweet–sour flavour that goes well with flavours such as vanilla, citrus and chocolate. Use them in sorbets, preserves, as toppings for meringue or in fillings for pastries or crepes.

Boysenberry pie

SERVES 6

sweet shortcrust pastry
400 g (14 oz/3¼ cups) plain (all-purpose)
    flour
180 g (6½ oz) cold unsalted butter, chopped
2 tablespoons caster (superfine) sugar
3–4 tablespoons iced water

filling
500 g (1 lb 2 oz/4 cups) boysenberries
    or blackberries
150 g (5½ oz/⅔ cup) caster (superfine)
    sugar
2 tablespoons cornflour (cornstarch)

milk, for brushing
1 egg, lightly beaten
caster (superfine) sugar, to sprinkle
cream or vanilla ice cream, to serve

To make the sweet shortcrust pastry, sift the flour and ¼ teaspoon salt into a large bowl. Using your fingertips, lightly rub the butter into the flour until the mixture resembles fine breadcrumbs. Fold in the sugar.

Make a well in the centre, add nearly all the water and mix with a flat-bladed knife, using a cutting rather than a stirring action. The mixture will come together in small beads of dough. If necessary, add more water, a teaspoon at a time, until the dough comes together. Test the dough by pinching a little piece between your fingers — if it doesn't hold together, it needs more water. Gather the dough together and lift out onto a lightly floured surface. Press the dough into a ball and then flatten it slightly. Cover in plastic wrap and refrigerate for 20–30 minutes.

Preheat the oven to 200°C (400°F/Gas 6). Grease a 26 x 20 cm (10¼ x 8 inch) pie dish. Roll out half the dough between two sheets of baking paper until it is large enough to fit into the dish. Remove the top sheet of paper and invert the pastry into the dish. Use a small ball of pastry to help press it down, allowing it to hang over the sides, then use a small knife to trim away the excess pastry.

To make the filling, toss the boysenberries, sugar and cornflour together in a bowl until well combined, then transfer to the pie dish. Roll out the remaining pastry between two sheets of baking paper until large enough to cover the pie. Moisten the rim of the pie base with a little milk and press the pastry lid firmly into place. Trim and crimp the edges. Brush with egg and sprinkle with a little caster sugar. Pierce the top of the pie with a knife.

Transfer to the bottom shelf of the oven and bake for 10 minutes, then reduce the oven temperature to 180°C (350°F/Gas 4) and move the pie to the centre shelf. Bake for another 30 minutes, or until golden on top. Cool a little before cutting into wedges and serving with cream or ice cream.

Polenta and sour cream pound cake with boysenberry compote

SERVES 10–12

150 g (5 1/2 oz) unsalted butter, softened
230 g (8 1/2 oz/1 cup) soft brown sugar
115 g (4 oz/ 1/2 cup) caster (superfine) sugar
5 eggs
185 g (6 1/2 oz/ 3/4 cup) sour cream
1/2 teaspoon natural almond extract
1 teaspoon natural vanilla extract
155 g (5 1/2 oz/1 1/4 cups) plain
    (all-purpose) flour
1 1/2 teaspoons baking powder
150 g (5 1/2 oz/1 cup) fine polenta
whipped cream, to serve

boysenberry compote
80 g (2 3/4 oz/ 1/3 cup) caster (superfine)
    sugar
2 teaspoons lemon juice
500 g (1 lb 2 oz/4 cups) boysenberries

Preheat the oven to 180°C (350°F/Gas 4). Grease a 24 x 14 cm (9 1/2 x 5 1/2 inch) loaf (bar) tin.

Using electric beaters, cream the butter, brown sugar and sugar in a large bowl until pale and fluffy. Add the eggs one at a time, beating well after each addition. Reduce the speed to low and mix in the sour cream and almond and vanilla extracts.

Sift together the flour, baking powder and a pinch of salt. Add the flour mixture and polenta to the butter mixture and gently stir to combine well. Spoon the batter into the prepared tin, smooth the surface, then bake for 50 minutes, or until a skewer inserted into the centre of the cake comes out clean. Cool in the tin for 5 minutes, then turn out onto a wire rack to cool completely.

Meanwhile, make the boysenberry compote. Put the sugar, lemon juice and 2 tablespoons water in a saucepan, then stir over medium heat for 3 minutes, or until the sugar has dissolved. Add the boysenberries, stir to coat, and bring the mixture to a simmer. Cook over medium–low heat for 5 minutes, stirring occasionally, or until the berries are soft but still holding their shape. Remove from the heat and cool to room temperature.

Cut the cake into thick slices and serve toasted, with the compote and cream.

For a quick dessert, stir **boysenberries** through whipped cream along with some ground almonds, soft brown sugar, lemon juice and vanilla extract, then spoon into wine or dessert glasses.

fig

With its velvety skin, rose-tinted, seedy flesh and delicate, sweet flavour, it's easy to understand why the ancients regarded the fig as food of the gods. The fig tree was known as the 'tree of life' by the Indians and ancient Egyptians, the leaves were mentioned in the bible story of Adam and Eve, and the fig was regarded by the Greeks as a symbol of fertility. Because of their high sugar content, figs were once used as a sweetener for food.

Varieties

There are hundreds of varieties of figs. Some of the most common are listed below.

Black genoa These large purple-skinned figs have sweet, pulpy, dark pink flesh.

Brown turkey A large fig with coppery brown skin, brownish pink flesh and a mild flavour.

Mission Also known as franciscan figs, these figs were introduced to California by the Franciscan missionaries. They are very firm figs with purple-black skin and pink flesh.

White adriatic These figs have a green skin, a flame-red interior and excellent flavour.

Buying and storing

- The peak season for figs is from summer to mid-autumn.

- While fig trees are very hardy, the fruit is very delicate. Figs must be picked when completely ripe because they won't ripen after picking. Choose figs that yield slightly to pressure but are not too squashy. Figs that are split or leaking are past their prime.

- Some figs may be coated in a light bloom: this is a sign that they are ready to eat.

- Store on a plate in the fridge for 2–3 days, but bring to room temperature before eating.

Preparation

Wipe figs lightly with a damp cloth before eating them. Always trim off the stem as this contains an oozy white substance, which is unpleasant to eat.

Some figs have thicker skins than others and need to be peeled — use a peeler to do this or simply use a small paring knife to pull the skin off, working from the stem down.

fig **107**

Fig and raspberry cake

SERVES 6–8

185 g (6$\frac{1}{2}$ oz) unsalted butter, softened
185 g (6$\frac{1}{2}$ oz/$\frac{3}{4}$ cup) caster (superfine)
   sugar
1 egg
1 egg yolk
335 g (11$\frac{3}{4}$ oz/2$\frac{2}{3}$ cups) plain
   (all-purpose) flour
1 teaspoon baking powder
4 fresh figs, quartered
200 g (7 oz/1$\frac{2}{3}$ cups) raspberries
finely grated zest of 1 orange
2 tablespoons caster (superfine) sugar, extra
cream or mascarpone cheese, to serve

Preheat the oven to 180°C (350°F/Gas 4). Lightly grease a 23 cm (9 inch) spring-form cake tin.

Cream the butter and sugar in a bowl until light and pale. Add the egg and egg yolk and beat again. Sift the flour and baking powder into the bowl and add a pinch of salt. Stir to combine. Chill for 15 minutes, or until the dough is firm enough to roll out.

Divide the dough in two equal halves and roll out one half large enough to fit the base of the tin. Arrange the figs and raspberries over the dough base and sprinkle over the orange zest. Roll out the remaining dough and place it over the filling. Lightly brush the top with water and sprinkle with sugar.

Bake for 30 minutes, or until a skewer inserted into the centre of the cake comes out clean. Cut into slices and serve with cream or mascarpone cheese.

Figs in honey syrup

SERVES 4–6

12 fresh figs
100 g (3$\frac{1}{2}$ oz/$\frac{2}{3}$ cup) blanched whole
   almonds, lightly toasted
110 g (3$\frac{3}{4}$ oz/$\frac{1}{2}$ cup) sugar
4 tablespoons honey
2 tablespoons lemon juice
6 cm (2$\frac{1}{2}$ inch) strip of lemon zest
1 cinnamon stick
250 g (9 oz/1 cup) Greek-style yoghurt

Cut the stems off the figs and make a small crossways incision 5 mm ($\frac{1}{4}$ inch) deep on top of each. Push a toasted almond into each fig, through the incision.

Pour 750 ml (26 fl oz/3 cups) water into a large saucepan, add the sugar and stir over medium heat until the sugar has dissolved. Increase the heat and bring to the boil.

Stir in the honey and lemon juice, then add the strip of lemon zest and the cinnamon stick. Reduce the heat to medium, add the figs and gently simmer for 10 minutes. Remove the figs with a slotted spoon and place in a serving dish.

Boil the liquid in the pan over high heat for 15–20 minutes, or until thick and syrupy, then discard the cinnamon and lemon zest. Allow the syrup to cool slightly, then pour over the figs.

Roughly chop the remaining almonds and sprinkle over the figs. Serve warm or cold, with the yoghurt.

Greek-style chicken with figs

SERVES 4

1.5 kg (3 lb 5 oz) chicken, cut into
    8 even-sized pieces
1 tablespoon olive oil
12 fresh figs (not too big), or 12 dried figs,
    soaked in hot water for 2 hours
10 garlic cloves
1 large onion, thinly sliced
$1/2$ teaspoon ground coriander
$1/2$ teaspoon ground cinnamon
$1/2$ teaspoon ground cumin
a pinch of cayenne pepper
3 bay leaves
375 ml (13 fl oz/$1^1/2$ cups) port
1 teaspoon finely grated lemon zest
2 tablespoons lemon juice

Preheat the oven to 180°C (350°F/Gas 4). Remove any excess fat from the chicken and reserve the chicken giblets if there are any. Lightly season the chicken with salt and pepper. Heat the olive oil in a large heavy-based frying pan over high heat and cook the chicken in batches, skin side down, for 5 minutes, or until the skin is golden.

Remove from the pan and place, skin side down, in a single layer in a baking tin with the giblets. Place the figs between the chicken pieces. Scatter the garlic cloves and onion over the top, carefully pressing them into any gaps and being careful not to squash the figs. Sprinkle the spices over the top, tuck in the bay leaves, then pour in the port.

Cover and bake for 25 minutes, then turn the chicken over. Uncover and bake for another 20 minutes. Stir in the lemon zest and juice and bake for another 15 minutes, or until the chicken is tender and cooked through.

Pork with quince and fig salad

SERVES 4

80 g ($2^3/4$ oz/$1/4$ cup) quince paste (from
    delicatessens or see recipe, page 76)
600 g (1 lb 5 oz) pork fillet
8 fresh figs, halved
1 teaspoon fennel seeds
50 g ($1^3/4$ oz) baby rocket (arugula) leaves
2 tablespoons olive oil
1 tablespoon balsamic vinegar

Preheat the grill (broiler) to medium. Mash the quince paste until smooth and rub all over the pork fillet. Place on a lightly oiled, foil-covered baking tray. Put the tray under the grill and cook the pork for 10 minutes, ensuring it is not too close to the heat source or the quince paste might burn. Turn the pork over and cook for a further 8–10 minutes, or until just cooked through. Remove the pork, cover loosely with foil and leave to rest.

While the pork is resting, sprinkle the figs evenly with the fennel seeds and grill (broil) for 3–5 minutes, or until softened. Remove from the heat and allow to cool. Slice the pork diagonally and gently toss in a large bowl with the figs, rocket, oil and vinegar. Season to taste with salt and freshly ground black pepper.

If you buy **figs** that don't have much flavour, cut them into quarters, drizzle with some honey and flash them under the grill (broiler). Top with some honeyed yoghurt and a scattering of crushed walnuts.

Figs are an excellent fruit source of calcium and they are packed with dietary fibre. Figs are also rich in potassium, phosphorus and iron.

Chicken stuffed with figs and fennel

SERVES 4

170 ml (5 1/2 fl oz/2/3 cup) olive oil
140 g (5 oz) smoked pancetta, diced
1 onion, chopped
1 fennel bulb, chopped
1 large potato, cut into 2 cm (3/4 inch) cubes
2 garlic cloves, chopped
1 tablespoon chopped rosemary
125 ml (4 fl oz/1/2 cup) white wine
finely grated zest of 1 large orange
4 fresh figs, chopped
2 kg (4 lb 8 oz) whole chicken

To make the stuffing, heat 4 tablespoons of the olive oil in a saucepan. Add the pancetta and onion and cook over medium–high heat, stirring often, for 5 minutes, or until golden. Add the fennel and potato and cook for another 2 minutes. Add the garlic and rosemary and season with salt and freshly ground black pepper. Stir in the wine, reduce the heat, then cover and cook for about 15 minutes, or until the potato is tender and has absorbed the wine. Remove the pan from the heat and add the orange zest and figs. Set aside to cool if not using immediately. The stuffing can be made several hours in advance and left in the fridge. (If you do this, allow another 10 minutes cooking time.)

Preheat the oven to 250°C (500°F/Gas 9). Season the cavity of the chicken, then fill with the stuffing. (If there is any stuffing left over, add it to the roasting tin 15 minutes before removing the chicken from the oven.)

Put the chicken, breast side up, in a roasting tin, drizzle over the remaining oil and cook for 15 minutes. Remove the chicken from the oven and turn it over, then cook for another 15 minutes. After this time, turn the chicken onto its back, reduce the oven temperature to 180°C (350°F/Gas 4) and cook for a further 30 minutes.

Check that the chicken is cooked by piercing the thickest part of the thigh with a skewer — the juices should run clear. Check that the stuffing is cooked through by pushing a skewer into the cavity for 3 seconds — the skewer should feel very hot when you pull it out. If it isn't, cover the chicken with foil and cook for a further 10–15 minutes, or until the stuffing is heated through.

Remove the chicken from the oven, cover with foil and rest for 10 minutes before serving. Serve with any extra stuffing and pour over any juices.

fig **111**

Figs go well with honey, walnuts, pistachios, yoghurt, citrus, rosewater, raspberries, and cheeses such as blue cheese and goat's cheese. Serve dried figs on a cheese platter along with some dried apricots and almonds.

Grilled figs in prosciutto

MAKES 12

25 g (1 oz) unsalted butter
1 tablespoon orange juice
12 small fresh figs
12 sage leaves
6 slices prosciutto, trimmed and halved
    lengthways

Put the butter in a small heavy-based saucepan. Melt the butter over low heat, then cook for 8–10 minutes, or until the froth subsides and the milk solids appear as brown specks on the bottom of the saucepan. Strain the butter through a sieve lined with paper towels into a clean bowl, then stir in the orange juice.

Wash the figs gently and pat them dry with paper towels. Cut each fig into quarters, starting from the stem end and cutting almost to the base, then gently open out — the figs will open like a flower. Put a sage leaf in the opening of each fig, then wrap a piece of prosciutto around each one, tucking the ends under the base of the fig. Arrange the figs, cut side up, in a shallow heatproof dish and brush with the butter mixture.

Put the figs under a hot grill (broiler) and cook for 1–2 minutes, or until the prosciutto is slightly crisp. Serve the figs warm or at room temperature.

fig 113

Buying and storing

- Gooseberries are in season during summer.

- Unlike most berries, gooseberries continue to ripen after picking. Choose firm berries with no signs of bruising.

- Store for 1–2 days at room temperature, or about 1 week in the fridge.

Preparation

Gooseberries need to be topped and tailed before cooking. Because of their high levels of vitamin C, potassium and citric acid — which accounts for their tartness — they generally need to be cooked with a fair amount of sugar to sweeten them, even for use in savoury dishes. If using them for smooth desserts or sauces, press them through a sieve after cooking to remove any skin and seeds.

gooseberry

Gooseberries are one of the few fruit that are generally not eaten raw. These tart berries range in colour from green to greenish red or yellow, and have opaque, finely veined skins, which can be either furry or smooth. Gooseberries are popular in the United Kingdom and Northern Europe where their pleasant acidity makes them perfect for cutting the richness of oily fish such as mackerel, duck or game meats, or in sweet tarts, sauces and desserts. High in pectin, gooseberries are ideal fruit for jams and conserves.

Gooseberry cream shortcake

SERVES 6–8

pastry
300 g (10 1/2 oz/2 1/2 cups) self-raising flour
80 g (2 3/4 oz/1/3 cup) caster (superfine)
   sugar
125 g (4 1/2 oz) unsalted butter, chopped
1 egg, lightly beaten

550 g (1 lb 4 oz/3 cups) gooseberries,
   topped and tailed
285 g (10 oz/1 1/4 cups) caster (superfine)
   sugar
150 g (5 1/2 oz/2/3 cup) cream cheese
60 g (2 1/4 oz/1/4 cup) sour cream
1 tablespoon plain (all-purpose) flour
1 egg yolk, mixed with 2 teaspoons water
whipped cream, to serve

To make the pastry, combine the flour and sugar in a large bowl and stir to mix well. Using your fingertips, lightly rub the butter into the flour until the mixture resembles coarse breadcrumbs. Add the egg and, using a fork, mix until a soft dough forms. Form the dough into a flat disc, cover with plastic wrap and refrigerate while you prepare the filling.

To make the filling, combine the gooseberries and 230 g (8 oz/1 cup) of the sugar in a saucepan. Bring to the boil over medium heat and cook, uncovered, for 10–15 minutes, or until the berries are cooked and the liquid is thick and syrupy. Remove the pan from the heat and cool.

Using an electric mixer or food processor, mix the cream cheese, sour cream and remaining sugar together until the mixture is smooth. Stir in the flour and egg yolk until combined.

Preheat the oven to 180°C (350°F/Gas 4). Lightly grease a 25 cm (10 inch) loose-based tart tin. On a lightly floured surface, roll out two-thirds of the pastry to cover the base and side of the tin. Press the pastry into the tin using a small ball of dough to help press it down, then use a small knife to trim away the excess pastry.

Spoon the gooseberry mixture into the tin, then spoon the cream cheese mixture over the berries. Roll out the remaining pastry on a floured surface to about 5 mm (1/4 inch) thick and cut into 1.5 cm (5/8 inch) strips. Arrange the strips on a slight diagonal over the top to form a lattice pattern, trimming and joining pieces of pastry as needed.

Brush the lattice strips with the egg yolk mixture, then bake for 35–40 minutes, or until the pastry is firm and golden. Cool, then serve warm or at room temperature with whipped cream.

Gently sauté sliced **gooseberries** with some sherry vinegar or balsamic vinegar, thyme and soft brown sugar, then serve with rich meats such as pan-fried duck breasts or pork chops.

grape

What could be more delightful than the simple pleasure of eating a bunch of chilled fresh grapes? Red or green, seeded or without, table grapes or wine grapes — grapes offer up endless ways to use them. Serve them with cheese and crackers, throw a handful into a chicken and watercress salad or toss them in a fruit salad.

Varieties

There are over 8000 grape varieties, although many of these are used for making wine rather than eating out of hand.

Thompson seedless This variety is often processed into raisins. They have yellowish green skin and a pronounced sweet flavour.

Flame seedless A dark red, seedless grape with a juicy flesh and slightly tart flavour.

Red globe This very large, round red grape has a subtle flavour, mealy flesh and a large seed.

Muscat An ancient grape, muscats are used for making wine, raisins and as a table fruit. There are many varieties, including the muscat of Alexandria, a very sweet, juicy large grape with yellowish skin; and muscat Hamburg, a medium–large dark blue grape with a pleasant, sweet wine-flavoured flesh.

Buying and storing

- The peak season for grapes is from mid-summer to early autumn.

- Grapes do not sweeten further after they've been picked, so make sure they are at their best when you buy them. Choose grapes that are plump and are still firmly attached to their stems — a gentle shake will show if the bunch is too old, as the grapes will fall off their stems.

- Green grapes should be pale yellow-green rather than grassy green, whereas red grapes are at their best when deeply coloured.

- Don't wash grapes before storage — it's impossible to thoroughly dry between them, and trapped water will dilute their flavour and cause them to deteriorate quickly.

- Store in a plastic bag in the fridge for about 1 week. Wash and pat dry just before eating.

Preparation

Peeling Although grapes don't usually need to be peeled, it may be necessary to do so if you want to use them in sauces, or if the skins are tough and tannic. To do this, cut a small incision at the stem end of the grape, then carefully peel the skin off. For grapes with thick skins, it may be easier to first blanch them in boiling water for 20 seconds or so, then refresh in iced water before peeling. To remove the seeds, cut the grape in half and pick them out.

Grape fritters with cinnamon sugar

MAKES 24

2 tablespoons caster (superfine) sugar
1 teaspoon ground cinnamon

fritters
2 eggs, separated
1/2 teaspoon natural vanilla extract
60 g (2 1/4 oz/1/4 cup) caster (superfine)
    sugar
150 g (5 1/2 oz/3/4 cup) large seedless red
    or black grapes
40 g (1 1/2 oz/1/3 cup) self-raising flour
40 g (1 1/2 oz) unsalted butter

To make the cinnamon sugar, combine the sugar and cinnamon in a bowl. Set aside.

To make the fritters, whisk the egg yolks with the vanilla and sugar until pale and creamy. Slice each grape into four and stir into the egg mixture. Sift the flour into the mixture and stir to combine. Beat the egg whites in a separate bowl until soft peaks form. Using a metal spoon, gently fold half the egg white into the grape mixture until just combined and then fold in the remaining egg white.

Melt a little butter in a frying pan over low heat. Drop 6 heaped teaspoons of the batter separately into the pan, and cook over low–medium heat for 2–3 minutes. When the base becomes firm and bubbles appear around the edges, carefully turn the fritters over and cook for a further 2 minutes, or until golden.

Remove to a plate and keep warm, covered, in a 120°C (235°F/Gas 1/2) oven. Repeat to make 24 fritters. Dust the fritters with the cinnamon sugar and serve immediately.

Sole veronique

SERVES 4

12 sole fillets
250 ml (9 fl oz/1 cup) fish stock
3 tablespoons white wine
1 French shallot, thinly sliced
1 bay leaf
6 black peppercorns
2 parsley sprigs
3 teaspoons butter
3 teaspoons plain (all-purpose) flour
125 ml (4 fl oz/1/2 cup) milk
3 tablespoons cream
125 g (4 1/2 oz) seedless green grapes,
    peeled

Preheat the oven to 180°C (350°F/Gas 4). Lightly grease a shallow ovenproof dish and put the fish fillets in the dish.

Combine the stock, wine, shallot, bay leaf, peppercorns and parsley and pour over the fish. Cover the dish with greased foil and bake for 15 minutes, or until the fish flakes when tested with a fork. Carefully lift the fish out of the liquid and transfer to another dish. Cover with foil and keep warm.

Pour the cooking liquid into a saucepan and boil for about 2 minutes, or until reduced by half, then strain through a fine sieve.

In a clean saucepan, melt the butter, then add the flour and stir for 1 minute, or until pale and foaming. Remove from the heat and gradually stir in the combined milk, cream and reduced cooking liquid. Return to the heat and stir until the mixture boils and thickens. Season with salt and pepper, add the grapes and then stir until heated through. Serve the sauce over the fish.

note You can substitute flounder for the sole.

Evidence suggests that not long after **grapes** were first found growing in the Middle East, people learned that their juice could be fermented into wine. Along with wine, grapes are also used to make vinegar, verjuice, jam, grapeseed oil and the leavening agent, cream of tartar. They are dried to make currants, raisins and sultanas, and the skins and seeds (left over from wine-making) are distilled to make the Italian brandy, grappa. This versatility makes them an extremely valuable crop, second only to olives as the most widely cultivated temperate-climate fruit.

Rocket, grape and walnut salad

SERVES 6

1 butter lettuce
1 radicchio
155 g (5 1/2 oz) rocket (arugula) leaves
180 g (6 oz/1 cup) seedless green grapes
60 g (2 1/4 oz/1/2 cup) roughly chopped
    toasted walnuts

dressing
4 tablespoons extra virgin olive oil
1 tablespoon lemon juice
2 teaspoons wholegrain mustard
1 tablespoon snipped chives

Discard the tough outer leaves from the lettuce and radicchio, then separate the remaining leaves. Gently wash the lettuce, radicchio and rocket, then dry thoroughly. Transfer the salad leaves to an airtight container or sealed plastic bag and chill in the fridge.

To make the dressing, put the olive oil, lemon juice and mustard in a bowl and whisk well to combine. Season with freshly ground black pepper and stir in the chives.

Put the chilled leaves in a large serving bowl with the grapes. Toss well, then scatter with the walnuts. Drizzle the dressing over the salad and serve.

Sweet grape flat bread

SERVES 6

100 g (3 1/2 oz/3/4 cup) raisins
90 ml (3 fl oz) sweet Marsala
150 ml (5 fl oz) milk
115 g (4 oz/1/2 cup) caster (superfine) sugar
7 g (1/4 oz or 2 teaspoons) dried yeast
300 g (10 1/2 oz/2 1/2 cups) plain
   (all-purpose) flour
olive oil
500 g (1 lb 2 oz/2 3/4 cups) seedless red
   or black grapes

Combine the raisins and Marsala in a bowl. Warm the milk and put in a small bowl. Stir in 1 teaspoon of the sugar, then sprinkle over the yeast and set aside in a draught-free place for 7 minutes, or until the mixture becomes foamy.

Put the flour, 90 g (3 1/4 oz/1/3 cup) of the sugar and a pinch of salt in a bowl and mix together. Add the yeast mixture and mix until a dough forms. Transfer to a lightly floured surface and knead for 6–8 minutes, or until the dough is smooth and elastic. Add a little more flour or a few drops of warm water if necessary to give a soft, but not sticky, dough.

Lightly oil the inside of a large bowl with olive oil, put the dough in the bowl and roll to coat in the oil. Cut a cross on the top of the dough with a knife. Cover with plastic wrap and leave the dough in a draught-free place for 1 hour, or until doubled in size.

Preheat the oven to 180°C (350°F/Gas 4). Drain the raisins and squeeze them dry. Lightly dust a baking tray with flour.

Punch down the dough and divide into two. Shape each half into a flattened round about 20 cm (8 inches) in diameter, and place one round on the tray. Scatter half the grapes and half the raisins over the dough, and then cover with the second round of dough. Scatter the remaining grapes and raisins over the top. Cover loosely with a tea towel and leave in a draught-free place for 1 hour, or until doubled in size.

Sprinkle the dough with the remaining sugar. Bake for 40–50 minutes, or until golden. Serve warm or at room temperature, cut into thick slices.

Unlike many fruit bearing that moniker, such as strawberries, **grapes** are actually true berries. Grapes contain vitamins B and C, dietary fibre, some potassium and protein. Added to this is resveratrol, a compound found in the skin of red grapes and in red wine. Some research suggests that resveratrol may have anticancer and antioxidant properties.

Buying and storing

- Raspberries are in season from late summer to early autumn.

- Check to see that the hulls have been removed when picked, which will leave the characteristic hollow centre. If the hull is still attached, this may mean that the berries were picked when underripe and will be sour.

- Avoid washing raspberries if you can (this is unavoidable if they have been sprayed), as they lose their flavour, although some growers may use organic farming methods, so check with your supplier. If you do need to wash them, do so just before you eat them.

- Raspberries are a delicate fruit and should be eaten soon after purchase. Store them in the fridge for up to 2 days, or freeze them for up to 3 months.

raspberry

Raspberries are undoubtedly one of the most delicately flavoured of the berries. Perhaps the best way to showcase their glorious colour and slightly tart flavour is to serve them simply topped with whipped cream, perhaps sweetened with a little sugar. Raspberries provide a good counterbalance for rich flavours, so are often teamed with white or dark chocolate in mousses, brownies and cakes; paired with almonds or hazelnuts; or used in sweet desserts such as meringues.

Raspberry flummery

SERVES 4

600 g (1 lb 5 oz) raspberries
230 g (8 oz/1 cup) caster (superfine) sugar
2¹/₂ teaspoons powdered gelatine
whipped cream, to serve

Put the raspberries and sugar in a saucepan
and crush the raspberries. Bring to the boil
and simmer for 2 minutes.

Put 4 tablespoons water in a bowl, sprinkle
the gelatine in an even layer over the surface
and leave to sponge. Stir the sponged
gelatine into the hot raspberries, stirring
to melt the gelatine.

Strain the mixture through a fine sieve into
a bowl. Pour into four glasses and refrigerate
overnight to set. Serve with whipped cream.

White chocolate and raspberry mousse

SERVES 4

150 g (5¹/₂ oz) white chocolate, chopped
150 ml (5 fl oz) cream
4 eggs, separated
250 g (9 oz/2 cups) raspberries, crushed
raspberries, extra, to serve

Melt the white chocolate in a heatproof bowl
over a saucepan of simmering water, making
sure that the water does not touch the base
of the bowl. Cool slightly, then stir in the
cream. Stir the egg yolks into the chocolate
and mix well.

Whisk the egg whites in a clean, dry bowl
until stiff peaks form. Fold a third of the egg
white into the chocolate mixture to loosen
them. Fold in the remaining egg white until
just combined.

Fold the raspberries into the mixture, then
divide among four serving bowls. Refrigerate
for at least 4 hours. Decorate with extra fresh
raspberries to serve.

Chargrilled chicken with spinach and raspberries

SERVES 4

2 tablespoons raspberry vinegar
2 tablespoons lime juice
2 garlic cloves, crushed
1 tablespoon chopped oregano
1 teaspoon soft brown sugar
2 small red chillies, finely chopped
3 tablespoons extra virgin olive oil
4 boneless, skinless chicken breasts
200 g (7 oz/4 1/2 cups) baby English spinach
   leaves
250 g (9 oz/2 cups) fresh raspberries

dressing
3 tablespoons extra virgin olive oil
1 tablespoon raspberry vinegar
1 tablespoon chopped oregano
1 teaspoon dijon mustard

In a large bowl, combine the vinegar, lime juice, garlic, oregano, brown sugar, chilli and olive oil. Add the chicken, turning to coat, then cover and refrigerate for 2 hours.

Preheat the oven to 180°C (350°F/Gas 4). Heat a chargrill pan or barbecue chargrill plate to medium–high. Add the chicken and cook for 3 minutes on each side.

Place the chicken breasts on a baking tray and transfer to the oven. Cook for 5 minutes, or until the chicken is just cooked through. Remove from the oven, cover the chicken loosely with foil and leave to rest in a warm place for 5 minutes. Carve each breast on the diagonal into five pieces.

Combine the dressing ingredients in a jar and season with 1/4 teaspoon sea salt and freshly ground black pepper, to taste.

Gently toss the spinach and raspberries in a serving bowl with half the dressing. Arrange the chicken over the top and drizzle with the remaining dressing.

Most **raspberries** are red, but there is also the rarer golden raspberry and a lesser-known black version. If you happen to come across yellow raspberries at your local grower's market, give them a try — they have a mild flavour and are a little sweeter than red raspberries.

Amaretti, pear and raspberry trifles

MAKES 4

170 g (6 oz/$^3/_4$ cup) caster (superfine) sugar
2 firm ripe pears, such as packham or
    williams, peeled, halved and cored
1 tablespoon sweet Marsala
2 teaspoons instant coffee granules
16 amaretti biscuits, roughly broken
2 tablespoons orange juice
200 g (7 oz/1$^2/_3$ cups) raspberries
vanilla ice cream, to serve

custard
420 ml (14$^1/_2$ fl oz/1$^2/_3$ cups) milk
2 tablespoons caster (superfine) sugar
1 teaspoon natural vanilla extract
2$^1/_2$ tablespoons custard powder

Put the sugar in a saucepan with 375 ml
(13 fl oz/1$^1/_2$ cups) water. Slowly bring the
mixture to a simmer, stirring occasionally to
dissolve the sugar. Add the pears and cook
over low–medium heat for 10 minutes, or
until the pears are tender. Drain the pears
well, discarding the syrup, and set aside.

To make the custard, put the milk, sugar and
vanilla in a heavy-based saucepan and bring
just to a simmer over low heat, stirring
occasionally. Mix the custard powder with
2 tablespoons water to form a smooth paste,
then whisk into the milk mixture until the
custard boils and thickens. Remove from the
heat and cover the surface directly with
plastic wrap to prevent a skin forming. Set
aside to cool.

Put the Marsala and coffee granules in a
small bowl and stir to dissolve the coffee.

Place the biscuits and orange juice in a large
bowl and stir to coat the biscuits. Layer half
the biscuits into the base of four serving
glasses and drizzle with the Marsala mixture.
Top with a third of the raspberries.

Roughly chop the pears and divide half of
them among the serving glasses. Pour in half
the custard. Repeat the layering, finishing with
the raspberries.

Chill the trifles for 10 minutes, or serve
immediately with vanilla ice cream.

For a simple **raspberry salad dressing**, push 100 g (3½ oz) raspberries through a sieve to remove the seeds (you will need about 2 tablespoons of purée). Whisk in 2 tablespoons lemon juice and 100 ml (3½ fl oz) olive oil and season with salt and pepper.

Duck breast with raspberries and cassis

SERVES 4

4 x 200 g (7 oz) duck breasts
2 teaspoons ground cinnamon
1 tablespoon raw (demerara) sugar
250 ml (9 fl oz/1 cup) red wine
150 ml (5 fl oz) crème de cassis
1 tablespoon cornflour (cornstarch)
   or arrowroot
250 g (9 oz/2 cups) raspberries

Using a sharp knife, score the duck breasts through the skin and fat, taking care not to cut into the meat.

Heat a frying pan over medium–high heat, add the duck breasts, skin side down, and cook for 4–5 minutes, until the skin browns and the fat runs out. Remove the duck from the pan and drain the excess fat. Leave the pan unwashed for later use.

In a small bowl, combine the cinnamon, sugar and 2 teaspoons sea salt. Sprinkle over the skin of the duck breasts, then press in with your hands. Season with freshly ground black pepper. Reheat the frying pan and cook

the duck breasts, skin side up, for 10 minutes, or until the duck is cooked through but still a little pink in the middle. Remove from the pan and leave to rest on a carving board. Set the pan aside, reserving about 2 tablespoons of cooking juices.

Meanwhile, mix together the wine and cassis in a jug. Pour about 100 ml (3½ fl oz) of the liquid into a small bowl and mix in the cornflour, then pour this back into the jug.

Return the pan with the cooking juices to the heat and pour in the red wine mixture. Simmer for 2–3 minutes, stirring constantly, until the sauce has thickened. Add the raspberries and simmer for another minute to warm the fruit through. Season to taste.

Preheat the grill (broiler) and cook the duck breasts, skin side up, for 1 minute, or until the sugar mixture starts to caramelise. Remove from the heat and slice the duck breasts thinly. Arrange on serving plates, pour a little of the hot sauce over the top and serve the rest of the sauce separately.

strawberry

Who can resist a bowl of freshly picked sun–ripened strawberries, or imagine the ritual of afternoon tea without scones slathered with strawberry jam and cream? Their fragrant sweetness and ruby-red colour can brighten both the taste and look of any meal; it's no wonder they are the most beloved of all summer berries.

Varieties

There are more than 600 strawberry varieties, ranging in colour from scarlet to yellow and even white. Along with cultivated strawberries, there are the smaller, sweeter wild strawberries. These are prized for their more intense flavour.

Strawberries belong to the rose family, so it's no surprise that adding a few drops of rosewater enhances their floral flavour. They are cultivated in temperate climates around the world and are unique in that the seeds grow around the outside of the fruit rather than inside.

Buying and storing

- Strawberries are available year-round but are best in summer and early autumn.
- Strawberries don't ripen further after picking; they just soften. Choose strawberries that are plump, fragrant and firm. Check the bottom of the container for mould or any strawberries that are leaking. Remove any mouldy ones if you see them, as the mould will soon spread to the others.
- Don't be tricked into thinking that the biggest or reddest strawberries are the tastiest; in fact, those that are smaller or have paler tips may be the sweetest.
- Store strawberries in the fridge in their container for 2–3 days, and bring to room temperature before serving. To freeze, first hull them, then freeze in a single layer on trays before transferring to a container.

Preparation

Don't wash strawberries before storing them as this dilutes their flavour, and hull them just before eating them. To 'hull' a strawberry means to remove the leafy top and stalk — pinch it off with your fingers or slice it off with a small knife.

Strawberry cheesecake muffins

MAKES 6

115 g (4 oz/$\frac{1}{2}$ cup) caster (superfine) sugar
4 tablespoons cream cheese, softened
250 g (9 oz/1$\frac{2}{3}$ cups) strawberries, hulled
1 tablespoon strawberry or orange-flavoured
  liqueur
175 g (6 oz/1$\frac{1}{3}$ cups) plain (all-purpose)
  flour
1 tablespoon baking powder
1 teaspoon finely grated orange zest
20 g ($\frac{3}{4}$ oz) unsalted butter, melted
1 egg
125 ml (4 fl oz/$\frac{1}{2}$ cup) milk
icing (confectioners') sugar, to dust

Preheat the oven to 180°C (350°F/Gas 4).
Lightly grease a 6-hole non-stick muffin tin.

Put half the sugar in a bowl, add the cream
cheese and mix together well. Set aside.

Set aside six small strawberries. Place the
remaining strawberries in a blender or food
processor along with the liqueur and
remaining sugar. Blend to a smooth sauce,
then strain through a fine sieve to remove the
strawberry seeds. Set the strawberry sauce
aside for serving.

Sift the flour, baking powder and $\frac{1}{2}$ teaspoon
salt into a large bowl, then stir in the orange
zest. In a separate bowl, beat the butter,
egg and milk together, then add to the dry
ingredients and mix until just combined —
do not overmix or the muffins will be tough.

Spoon half the batter into the muffin holes,
then add a reserved strawberry and a
teaspoon of the cream cheese mixture to
each one. Divide the remaining batter among
the holes. Transfer to the oven and bake for
15 minutes, or until the muffins are cooked
through and golden. To test if the muffins are
cooked, insert a skewer into one, avoiding the
cream cheese mixture — the skewer should
withdraw clean.

Remove the muffins from the tin and allow
to cool slightly. Serve dusted with icing sugar
and drizzled with the strawberry sauce. The
strawberry cheesecake muffins are best
eaten the day they are made.

Strawberries contain more vitamin C than oranges, and
are a good source of potassium and folic acid. They also
contain ellagic acid, a compound that is thought to have
anticancer properties. Note that strawberries can cause an
allergic reaction in babies, so wait until they are over one
year old before introducing them to the fruit.

Balsamic strawberries

SERVES 6

500 g (1 lb 2 oz/3 1/3 cups) strawberries,
    hulled and halved
3 tablespoons balsamic vinegar
2 tablespoons caster (superfine) sugar
2 teaspoons lemon juice
1 small handful mint leaves
vanilla ice cream, to serve

Strawberry curd

MAKES 500 ML (17 FL OZ/2 CUPS)

250 g (9 oz/1 2/3 cups) strawberries, hulled
    and roughly chopped
185 g (6 1/2 oz/3/4 cup) caster (superfine)
    sugar
125 g (4 1/2 oz) unsalted butter, softened
1 teaspoon finely grated lemon zest
1 tablespoon lemon juice
4 egg yolks

Put the strawberries in a glass bowl. Combine
the balsamic vinegar, sugar and lemon juice
in a small saucepan and stir over medium
heat for 5 minutes, or until the sugar
dissolves. Remove from the heat and cool.

Pour the cooled balsamic mixture over the
strawberries, add the mint leaves and toss
together. Cover with plastic wrap and
refrigerate for 1 hour to allow the flavours
to develop. Serve with vanilla ice cream.

Put the strawberries in a saucepan with the
sugar, butter, lemon zest and lemon juice.
Stir over low heat until the butter has melted
and the sugar has dissolved. Simmer gently
for 5 minutes, then remove the pan from
the heat.

Lightly beat the egg yolks in a large bowl,
then, stirring constantly, slowly add the
strawberry mixture in a thin stream. The
mixture will thicken as you add it.

Return the strawberry mixture to the pan and
place over low heat. Cook for 2 minutes,
stirring constantly. Don't allow the mixture to
boil or the curd will separate. Pour into hot
sterilised jars (see page 24) and seal.

The strawberry curd will keep in the fridge
for up to 2 months. Once opened, the curd
will keep for up to 5 days, refrigerated.

For a simple **strawberry filling**
for sponge cakes or a topping for
pavlova, crush some strawberries
with caster (superfine) sugar and
a dash of rosewater, then fold
through whipped cream.

Although their common name comes from the fact that **strawberries** were originally grown on straw, their botanical name, *Fragaria*, means 'fragrance', and perfectly describes their soft perfume. Strawberries had romantic associations long before they became synonymous with St Valentine's Day. Once regarded as an aphrodisiac in rural France, they are also the symbol of Venus, goddess of love, due to their red colour and heart shape.

Doughnut balls with strawberry sauce

SERVES 4–6

strawberry sauce
300 g (10½ oz/2 cups) fresh or thawed
    frozen strawberries
160 g (5½ oz/½ cup) strawberry jam

215 g (7½ oz/1¾ cups) self-raising flour
2 eggs
2 tablespoons olive oil
80 g (2¾ oz/⅓ cup) caster (superfine)
    sugar, plus extra for coating
vegetable oil, for deep-frying
ice cream, to serve (optional)

To make the strawberry sauce, put the strawberries and jam in a food processor and blend until smooth. Set aside.

Sift the flour into a bowl. In another bowl, whisk together the eggs, olive oil, sugar and 2 tablespoons water until smooth. Stir in the flour and mix to a soft dough. Using floured hands, roll 2 teaspoons of the batter into a ball, then repeat with the remaining batter.

Fill a wide heavy-based saucepan one-third full of oil and heat to 180°C (350°F), or until a cube of bread dropped into the oil browns in 15 seconds. Deep-fry the doughnuts in batches for 5–6 minutes, or until cooked through and lightly browned, using tongs to turn them once or twice during cooking. Transfer each batch to paper towels to drain. While still hot, roll them in the extra sugar to coat.

Serve the doughnuts hot with the strawberry sauce, and with ice cream if desired.

Strawberry and mascarpone tart

SERVES 6

185 g (6$\frac{1}{2}$ oz/1$\frac{1}{2}$ cups) plain (all-purpose)
    flour
125 g (4$\frac{1}{2}$ oz) cold unsalted butter, chopped
4 tablespoons iced water
500 g (1 lb 2 oz/3$\frac{1}{3}$ cups) strawberries,
    hulled and halved
2 teaspoons natural vanilla extract
50 ml (1$\frac{1}{2}$ fl oz) orange-based liqueur such
    as Cointreau or Grand Marnier
4 tablespoons soft brown sugar
250 g (9 oz) mascarpone cheese
300 ml (10 fl oz) thick (double/heavy) cream
2 teaspoons finely grated orange zest

Sift the flour and a pinch of sea salt into a large bowl. Using your fingertips, lightly rub the butter into the flour until the mixture resembles fine breadcrumbs. Make a well in the centre, then add almost all the iced water to the well. Mix using a flat-bladed knife until a rough dough forms, adding the remaining water if necessary. Gently gather the dough together, transfer to a lightly floured surface, then press into a round disc. Cover with plastic wrap and refrigerate for 30 minutes, or until firm.

Preheat the oven to 200°C (400°F/Gas 6) and place a baking tray in the oven to heat. Lightly grease a 23 cm (9 inch) loose-based tart tin.

Roll the dough out between two sheets of baking paper until large enough to line the tin. Trim the excess pastry using a small knife, then place the pastry-lined tin in the fridge and chill for 15 minutes.

Line the pastry shell with baking paper and half-fill with baking beads or rice. Place the tart tin on the heated tray in the oven and bake for 15 minutes, then remove the paper and baking beads and bake for a further 10–15 minutes, or until the pastry is dry and golden. Remove from the oven and allow to cool completely.

In a bowl, combine the strawberries, vanilla, liqueur and 1 tablespoon of the brown sugar. In another bowl, combine the mascarpone, cream, orange zest and remaining sugar. Cover both bowls and place in the fridge for 30 minutes, gently tossing the strawberries once or twice.

Whip half the mascarpone mixture until firm, then evenly spoon it into the pastry shell. Drain the strawberries, reserving the liquid, then pile the strawberries onto the tart.

Slice the tart and serve with a drizzle of the reserved strawberry liquid and the remaining mascarpone cream.

stone fruit

apricot

Originally from China, apricots are now grown in most temperate climates. They are excellent when eaten raw or in fruit salads but they also cook beautifully in jams, pies or tarts. Their rich flavour complements savoury dishes, and they are used widely in Middle Eastern cooking, particularly in lamb, chicken and rice dishes.

Buying and storing

- Like most stone fruit, apricots are in season during summer.

- Buying apricots from your local grower's market means you'll be buying apricots that have been sun-ripened and recently picked — their flavour is hard to beat.

- Choose fruit that are firm but not hard, and those with no bruises. They should feel slightly soft when pressed and have a faintly sweet fragrance, and a deep orange colour.

- The flavour of apricots may improve a little if stored at cool room temperature for a few days. Store in a single layer on a few layers of paper towel.

- Apricots are best eaten a day or two after you buy them, but will keep for up to 1 week in the fridge.

- If you are blessed with a glut of apricots, they are well suited to being bottled in syrup.

Preparation

Apricots don't need to be peeled before use as their smooth, thin skins are quite edible. They neatly split in half along their natural crease, and their stones can then be slipped out. The flesh will oxidise (turn brown) on contact with the air, so work quickly. If serving them raw, prepare them just before you plan to serve them or brush them with a little lemon juice to prevent this from occurring.

Apricot meringue torte

SERVES 8–10

375 g (13 oz/1²/₃ cups) caster (superfine)
  sugar
1 cinnamon stick
2 teaspoons natural vanilla extract
450 g (1 lb) apricots, quartered and stones
  removed (about 9 apricots)
6 egg whites, at room temperature
1¹/₂ teaspoons white vinegar
35 g (1¹/₄ oz/¹/₃ cup) ground hazelnuts
300 ml (10¹/₂ fl oz) whipping cream
icing (confectioners') sugar, to dust

Combine 375 ml (13 fl oz/1¹/₂ cups) water, 125 g (4¹/₂ oz/heaped ¹/₂ cup) of the sugar, the cinnamon stick and 1 teaspoon of the vanilla in a large saucepan. Stir over low heat until the sugar has dissolved, then increase the heat and simmer for 15 minutes. Add the quartered apricots and simmer over low heat for another 20 minutes, or until very soft. Set aside to cool.

Preheat the oven to 150°C (300°F/Gas 2). Draw a 22 cm (8¹/₂ inch) circle on two sheets of baking paper. Put the sheets, pencil side down, on two baking trays.

Using electric beaters, whisk the egg whites in a clean, dry bowl until stiff peaks form. Add the remaining sugar, a little at a time, and continue beating until the mixture is stiff and glossy. Beat in the vinegar and remaining vanilla. Gently fold in the ground hazelnuts.

Divide the meringue mixture between the two circles on the prepared trays and smooth the surface. Bake for 35–40 minutes, or until the meringues are firm and dry. Turn off the oven and leave the meringues in the oven to cool completely.

Peel off the baking paper and place one meringue on a serving plate. Whip the cream until stiff peaks form. Discard the cinnamon stick from the syrup and drain the apricots. Gently stir the apricots through the whipped cream and then spread over the meringue base. Put the second meringue on top of the apricot cream. Dust with icing sugar before cutting into wedges to serve.

Apricots go well with nuts such as almonds, hazelnuts and pistachios, and with flavours such as vanilla, rosemary, honey, saffron, dessert wines, rosewater and orange-flower water. Make a simple dessert by lightly poaching apricots in a syrup spiked with one or two of these flavours.

Apricot stones can be cracked open to obtain the kernel. These look similar to an almond and, when blanched and used sparingly, impart a delicious bitter almond flavour in jams and stewed or poached apricots. Take care, however, as the kernels contain hydrocyanic acid, which can be toxic if eaten in any quantity, so only use a few — 4 kernels in a large batch of jam or 3 in poached fruit to serve 6 to 8 people — and remove them before serving.

Apricot jam

MAKES 750 ML (26 FL OZ/3 CUPS)

1 kg (2 lb 4 oz) apricots (about 20)
1 kg (2 lb 4 oz/4 1/2 cups) sugar, warmed

Halve the apricots and remove the stones. Put the apricots in a large saucepan with 375 ml (13 fl oz/1 1/2 cups) water. Bring to the boil, stirring, for 20 minutes, or until the fruit has softened.

Meanwhile, warm the sugar slightly by first spreading it in a large baking tin and then heating it in a 120°C (235°F/Gas 1/2) oven for 10 minutes, stirring occasionally. Put two small plates in the freezer.

Add the warmed sugar to the pan and stir, without boiling, for 5 minutes, or until all the sugar has dissolved. Return to the boil and boil for 20 minutes, stirring often. Remove any scum during cooking with a slotted spoon. When the jam falls from a wooden spoon in thick sheets without dripping, start testing for setting point.

To do this, remove the pan from the heat. Put a little of the jam onto one of the cold plates and return the plate to the freezer for 30 seconds. A skin will form on the surface and the jam will wrinkle when pushed with your finger. If not, return to the heat for a few minutes and retest with the other plate.

Transfer the jam to a heatproof jug and immediately pour into hot sterilised jars (see page 24), and seal. Turn the jars upside down for 2 minutes, then turn back up again and leave to cool. Label and date for storage.

Store in a cool, dark place for 6–12 months. Once opened, the jam will keep in the fridge for 6 weeks.

Chicken with apricots and honey

SERVES 4

40 g (1½ oz) unsalted butter
1 teaspoon ground cinnamon
1 teaspoon ground ginger
a pinch of cayenne pepper
½ teaspoon freshly ground black pepper
4 x 175 g (6 oz) boneless, skinless chicken
    breasts, trimmed
1 onion, thinly sliced
250 ml (9 fl oz/1 cup) chicken stock
6 coriander (cilantro) sprigs, tied in a bunch,
    plus extra sprigs to garnish
500 g (1 lb 2 oz) apricots, halved and
    stones removed
2 tablespoons honey
2 tablespoons slivered almonds, toasted
steamed couscous, to serve

Melt the butter in a large frying pan. Add the spices and stir over low heat for 1 minute, or until fragrant. Increase the heat to medium and add the chicken. Cook for 1 minute on each side, taking care not to let the spices burn. Remove the chicken from the pan.

Add the onion to the frying pan and sauté for 5 minutes, or until softened. Return the chicken to the pan, add the stock and tied coriander sprigs and season with sea salt and freshly ground black pepper. Reduce the heat to low, then cover and simmer for 5 minutes, turning the chicken once.

Transfer the chicken to a serving dish, then cover and leave to rest for 2–3 minutes.

Meanwhile, put the apricots, cut side down, into the pan juices and drizzle with the honey. Cover and simmer for 7–8 minutes, turning the apricots after 5 minutes. Remove the coriander sprigs and discard them.

Spoon the apricots and sauce over the chicken, scatter the almonds over the top and garnish with a few extra coriander sprigs. Serve with steamed couscous.

cherry

Cherries are one of the few fruit that remain truly seasonal, making them all the more special when they appear each summer. With a divinely sweet, juicy flesh, cherries are best eaten out of hand, but also lend themselves to myriad sweet dishes such as black forest cake, sour cherry strudel and clafoutis, to name a few.

Varieties

Cherries can be broadly grouped into three types: sweet, sour and hybrid. Sweet cherries can be eaten raw or cooked and include varieties such as the bing (large and very dark red-black fruit), napoleon, florence and ranier (these three have yellowish skins that turn pink when ripe). Hybrids such as duke cherries can be used for both eating and cooking.

Sour cherries, such as maraschino and morello, are usually cooked in pies and cakes such as black forest cake and sour cherry strudel, or used in jams, and liqueurs such as kirsch.

Buying and storing

- Cherries are in season during summer.

- Always take the time to pick out the best cherries from the pile. Choose unblemished, shiny, large fruit that are heavy (cherries gain 30 per cent of their flavour and volume in the week before picking) and with no soft, wrinkled or spotted patches. Generally, the deeper the skin colour, the riper the fruit.

- Buy cherries with the stalks still on — they'll keep for longer. The stalks should be soft and pliable: brown, brittle stalks indicate the cherries are old. Use those without their stalks first.

- Sweet cherries will store for up to 3 days in a plastic bag in the fridge. Sour cherries will keep for up to 2 weeks in the fridge. Both sweet and sour types freeze well.

Cherry clafoutis

SERVES 6–8

Clafoutis is a harvest dish from France, often baked during cherry season. Traditionally, but perhaps unwisely, the cherry stones are left in. The stones add a mild bitter-almond flavour during cooking, but you can use pitted cherries if you prefer.

30 g (1 oz) unsalted butter, melted
500 g (1 lb 2 oz) cherries, pitted if preferred
60 g (2 1/4 oz/1/2 cup) self-raising flour
4 tablespoons sugar
2 eggs, lightly beaten
250 ml (9 fl oz/1 cup) milk
icing (confectioners') sugar, to dust
whipped cream or ice cream, to serve

Preheat the oven to 180°C (350°F/Gas 4). Brush a 23 cm (9 inch) glass or ceramic shallow pie dish with a little of the melted butter. Spread the cherries in the dish in a single layer.

Sift the flour into a bowl, add the sugar and make a well in the centre. Combine the eggs, milk and remaining butter, then gradually pour this into the well, whisking until just combined — do not overbeat or the batter will be tough.

Pour the batter over the cherries and bake for 40 minutes. Remove from the oven and dust liberally with icing sugar. Serve with cream or ice cream.

note Clafoutis is sometimes made using other stone fruit such as apricots or plums, or with apples.

Cherries are rich in antioxidants, which help to prevent cancer, plus abundant quantities of melatonin, which helps regulate the body's circadian rhythms. In fact, eating cherries is being credited with everything from helping to ease arthritis and gout to preventing diabetes and heart disease.

Cherry and cream cheese strudel

SERVES 8

250 g (9 oz/1 cup) cream cheese, softened
100 ml (3 1/2 fl oz) whipping cream
1 tablespoon brandy or cherry brandy
1 teaspoon natural vanilla extract
100 g (3 1/2 oz/scant 1/2 cup) caster
    (superfine) sugar
4 tablespoons ground almonds
4 tablespoons dry breadcrumbs
10 sheets ready-made filo pastry
75 g (2 1/2 oz) unsalted butter, melted
400 g (14 oz) cherries, pitted
icing (confectioners') sugar, for dusting

Preheat the oven to 200°C (400°F/Gas 6).
Lightly grease a large baking tray.

Put the cream cheese, cream, brandy, vanilla
and 3 tablespoons of the sugar in a bowl and
beat using electric beaters until smooth.

In another bowl, mix together the almonds,
breadcrumbs and remaining sugar.

Lay a sheet of filo pastry on a work surface
and cover the remaining sheets with a damp
tea towel so they don't dry out. Brush the
filo pastry with some of the melted butter
and sprinkle with some of the breadcrumb
mixture. Lay another sheet of filo pastry on
top, brush with more butter and sprinkle
with more breadcrumbs. Repeat with the
remaining filo and breadcrumbs.

Spread the cream cheese mixture evenly
over the pastry, leaving a 4 cm (1 1/2 inch)
border all around. Arrange the cherries over
the cream cheese, then brush some melted
butter over the pastry border.

Roll the pastry in from one long side, folding
in the ends as you roll. Form into a firm roll
and place on the baking tray, seam side
down. Brush all over the pastry with the
remaining butter.

Transfer the tray to the oven and bake for
10 minutes, then reduce the oven to 180°C
(350°F/Gas 4) and bake for 30 minutes, or
until the pastry is crisp and golden. Remove
from the oven and leave to cool on a wire
rack for a few minutes.

To serve, dust liberally with icing sugar and
cut into slices using a sharp serrated knife.
Serve warm.

date

Fresh dates have a sugar content of around 60 per cent and are one of the world's oldest food crops. Besides the sweet uses for dates in scones, cakes and muffins, they also feature in savoury dishes such as salads, tagines, sauces, rice and couscous. The Greek word *daktulos*, meaning 'finger', is thought to be the origin of its name, and refers to the shape of the fruit.

Varieties

There are many varieties of dates; they are rarely sold by name but the two you are most likely to see are medjool, a crinkly-skinned sticky date with a mellow sweet flavour, and the highly prized deglet noor, meaning 'date of light', which has a translucent, smooth skin, a chewy texture and delicate flavour.

Usually dates are sold by type: soft, semi-dry or dry. Soft dates are very fresh and have a high moisture content and fairly low sugar levels. Semi-dry dates (often erroneously labelled as 'fresh dates') have firmer but still soft flesh, lower moisture levels than soft dates but a higher sugar content. These have been partially dried to develop the sugars and extend their shelf-life. Dry, or 'bread', dates are quite hard and contain little moisture and lots of sugar. These are usually sold in packets and are often used as ingredients in baked goods.

Buying and storing

- The peak season for fresh dates is from autumn to winter.

- If possible, buy dates that aren't sold wrapped in plastic on a tray, as it's difficult to judge their condition. Hold the dates up to the light to see if their skins are translucent — an indication that they are fresh.

- Choose dates that are plump, with unbroken, slightly wrinkled skins. Avoid any with sugary surfaces — this means they are not fresh as their sugars are starting to crystallise.

- Store fresh dates at room temperature or in an airtight container in the fridge. Store dried dates in an airtight container in a cool, dark place, or in the fridge.

Sticky date pudding with caramel sauce

SERVES 6–8

370 g (13 oz/2 cups) fresh dates
1 1/2 teaspoons bicarbonate of soda
   (baking soda)
1 teaspoon grated ginger
90 g (3 1/4 oz) unsalted butter, softened
250 g (9 oz/heaped 1 cup) caster
   (superfine) sugar
3 eggs
185 g (6 1/2 oz/1 1/2 cups) self-raising flour
1/2 teaspoon mixed (pumpkin pie) spice
crème fraîche, to serve

caramel sauce
150 g (5 1/2 oz) unsalted butter, chopped
230 g (8 oz/1 1/4 cups) soft brown sugar
4 tablespoons golden syrup or maple syrup
185 ml (6 fl oz/3/4 cup) cream

Preheat the oven to 180°C (350°F/Gas 4). Grease a deep 23 cm (9 inch) round spring-form cake tin and line the base with baking paper.

Chop the dates and put them in a saucepan with 430 ml (15 fl oz/1 3/4 cups) water. Bring to the boil, then remove from the heat, add the bicarbonate of soda and ginger and leave to stand for 5 minutes.

Using electric beaters, cream together the butter, sugar and 1 egg. Beat in the remaining eggs one at a time, mixing well after each addition. Fold in the sifted flour and mixed spice, add the date mixture and stir until well combined. Pour into the prepared tin and bake for 55–60 minutes, or until a skewer inserted into the centre of the pudding comes out clean. Cover with foil if the pudding starts to brown too much during cooking. Leave to stand for 5 minutes before turning out onto a serving plate.

To make the caramel sauce, stir all the ingredients in a saucepan over low heat until the sugar has dissolved. Simmer, uncovered, for about 3 minutes, or until thickened slightly. Brush some sauce over the top and sides of the pudding. Serve with extra sauce and a dollop of crème fraîche.

Although now grown worldwide, the **date palm** is native to the Middle East where its fruit is held in high esteem. Legendarily the palm has 800 uses — the sap is drunk, the fibre is woven, the stones are ground and used for camel fodder, the palm-hearts are eaten and the bark is used as building material, to name a few.

Date pancakes with chocolate fudge sauce

MAKES 10–12 PANCAKES

185 g (6½ oz/1 cup) pitted dried dates,
  chopped
1 teaspoon bicarbonate of soda
  (baking soda)
250 g (9 oz/2 cups) self-raising flour
95 g (3¼ oz/½ cup) soft brown sugar
250 g (9 oz/1 cup) sour cream, softened
3 eggs, separated
melted butter, for brushing
ice cream, to serve

chocolate fudge sauce
250 g (9 oz/1⅔ cups) chopped
  dark chocolate
185 ml (6 fl oz/¾ cup) cream
50 g (1¾ oz) unsalted butter
1 tablespoon golden syrup or maple
  syrup
2 tablespoons Bailey's Irish Cream,
  Tia Maria or Kahlua

Put the dates in a small saucepan with
250 ml (9 fl oz/1 cup) water. Bring to the
boil, remove from the heat and stir in the
bicarbonate of soda. Leave to cool for
5 minutes. Transfer the mixture to a food
processor and purée until smooth, then set
aside to cool. Sift the flour into a large bowl.
Stir in the brown sugar and the date purée.

In a bowl, whisk together the sour cream and
egg yolks, then add to the flour mixture and
stir until smooth. Set aside for 15 minutes.

In a clean, dry bowl, beat the egg whites
using electric beaters until soft peaks form.
Stir a heaped tablespoon of egg white into
the batter to loosen it, then fold in the
remaining egg white until just combined.

Heat a frying pan over medium heat and
brush lightly with melted butter. Pour 60 ml
(2 fl oz/¼ cup) of batter into the pan. Cook
for 2–3 minutes, or until bubbles form on
the surface, then flip the pancake over and
cook the other side for 2 minutes, or until
the pancakes are golden and cooked
through. Transfer to a warmed plate and
cover with a tea towel while you cook the
remaining batter, brushing the pan with more
melted butter as necessary. Stack the cooked
pancakes between sheets of baking paper to
prevent them sticking together.

To make the chocolate fudge sauce, put the
chocolate, cream, butter and golden syrup
in a saucepan. Stir over low heat until the
chocolate has melted and the mixture is
smooth. Stir in the liqueur.

Serve the pancakes with ice cream, drizzled
with the sauce.

Trout stuffed with dates

SERVES 4

4 medium-sized trout
140 g (5 oz/1 cup) chopped fresh dates
45 g (1^1/$_2$ oz/^{1}/$_4$ cup) cooked rice
1 onion, finely chopped
4 tablespoons chopped coriander (cilantro)
^{1}/$_4$ teaspoon ground ginger
^{1}/$_4$ teaspoon ground cinnamon
50 g (1^3/$_4$ oz/^{1}/$_3$ cup) roughly chopped
    blanched almonds
40 g (1^1/$_2$ oz) butter, softened
ground cinnamon, to dust

Preheat the oven to 180°C (350°F/Gas 4).
Rinse the trout under cold running water and
pat dry with paper towels. Season with sea
salt and freshly ground black pepper.

Combine the dates, rice, half the onion, the
coriander, ginger, cinnamon, almonds and
half the butter in a bowl. Season well.

Spoon the stuffing into the fish cavities and
put each fish on a well-greased double sheet
of foil. Brush the fish with the remaining
butter and divide the remaining onion among
the four parcels. Wrap the fish neatly and seal
the edges of the foil by folding them over a
few times. Put the parcels on a large baking
tray and bake for 15–20 minutes, or until
cooked through. Serve dusted with cinnamon.

Date and cinnamon squares

MAKES 36

600 g (1 lb 5 oz/3^1/$_3$ cups) pitted dried
    dates, chopped
1 teaspoon bicarbonate of soda
    (baking soda)
125 g (4^1/$_2$ oz) unsalted butter, chopped
155 g (5^1/$_2$ oz/^{2}/$_3$ cup) soft brown sugar
2 eggs
125 g (4^1/$_2$ oz/1 cup) plain (all-purpose)
    flour
60 g (2^1/$_4$ oz/^{1}/$_2$ cup) self-raising flour
^{1}/$_2$ teaspoon ground cinnamon,
    plus ^{1}/$_2$ teaspoon, extra
60 g (2^1/$_4$ oz/^{1}/$_2$ cup) icing (confectioners')
    sugar

Preheat the oven to 180°C (350°F/Gas 4).
Lightly grease a 23 cm (9 inch) square cake
tin and line the base with baking paper. Put
the dates and 500 ml (17 fl oz/2 cups) water
in a saucepan, bring to the boil, then remove
from the heat. Stir in the bicarbonate of soda
and mix well. Cool to room temperature.

Cream the butter and sugar in a large bowl
using electric beaters until pale and fluffy.
Add the eggs one at a time, beating well after
each addition. Sift the flours and cinnamon
into a bowl, then fold into the butter mixture
alternately with the date mixture. Spread into
the prepared tin. Bake for 55–60 minutes, or
until a skewer inserted into the centre comes
out clean. Cool in the tin for 5 minutes, then
turn out onto a wire rack to cool completely.

Cut into 36 pieces and place on a sheet of
baking paper. Sift the combined icing sugar
and extra cinnamon over the top and toss
to coat. Serve immediately (the coating will
absorb into the cakes if left to stand).

- Peaches and nectarines are in season from summer to mid-autumn.

- Peaches and nectarines spoil quickly so only buy as many as needed. Choose fruit that give slightly to gentle pressure but don't feel too soft. Peaches in particular should have a mildly sweet fragrance, which indicates they are ripe.

- Both peaches and nectarines will soften at room temperature but won't ripen once they are picked.

- Store for up to 3 days at room temperature unless they are already very ripe. If stored in the fridge, bring back to room temperature before serving, as they are less flavoursome when chilled.

peach & nectarine

There could be no better symbol of summer than a perfectly ripe fragrant peach or nectarine eaten out of sticky hands. If they are to be cooked, peaches and nectarines are best suited to sweet recipes, although they do suit a few savoury dishes such as chutneys, salsas and salads. These fruit are well complemented by the flavours of almonds, champagne, vanilla, raspberries, wine, dashes of cinnamon or cardamom, yoghurt and cream.

Nectarine comes from the Greek *nektar*, meaning 'sweet', while '**peach**' is a corruption of the Latin *persica*, meaning 'Persian'. Both fruit are thought to have originated in China, where they are a symbol for long life.

Varieties

In general, mid-to-late summer peach and nectarine varieties taste better than those first fruits of summer. While there are dozens of types cultivated commercially, these are usually not sold by variety. Instead, these fruit are often divided into two groups, depending on whether the flesh clings to the stone or not.

Freestone As the name implies, these separate easily from their stone — all you need to do is cut through to the stone, all the way around the fruit, then gently twist the cut halves in opposite directions and pull them off the stone. Freestone (or slipstone) fruits are perfect for poaching whole halves or if you want to roast, stuff or bake intact halves. For bottling large quantities or making preserves, buy freestone fruits for ease of preparation.

Clingstone Clingstones will not yield their stones at all, so you need to cut the flesh away from the stone. Use clingstones if you want to serve whole poached peaches, or if you only need a purée or similar, where you don't need neat halves.

Preparation

Nectarines don't need to be peeled, but peaches with very fuzzy skins do, especially if served poached or in pies or jams.

To peel clingstones, score a cross at the base of each peach and put into a bowl of boiling water for 15–20 seconds. Using a slotted spoon, transfer to a bowl of iced water. When cool, peel off the skin. To peel freestones, score the peach through the skin all the way around and right through to the stone, then put into boiling water and then iced water, and peel, as above.

Prepare the fruit as needed, as the flesh can turn brown on contact with the air. Sprinkle the flesh with a little lemon juice to stop this.

What's the difference?

Nectarines are a subspecies of the peach and not, as is often thought, a cross between a peach and a plum — basically, the nectarine is a fuzz-free peach. Nectarine and peach trees are virtually indistinguishable from each other; in fact, no more than a single recessive gene (the one for 'fuzzlessness') separates the two fruit. Nectarines and peaches come with either white or yellow flesh, but the white-fleshed ones are often considered to be the best eating.

Poached vanilla peaches
with raspberry purée and passionfruit sauce

SERVES 4

350 g (12 oz/1 1/2 cups) caster (superfine)
   sugar
1 vanilla bean, halved lengthways
4 freestone peaches
100 g (3 1/2 oz/heaped 3/4 cup) raspberries
4 scoops vanilla ice cream

passionfruit sauce
4 tablespoons passionfruit pulp (from
   about 4 passionfruit)
2 tablespoons caster (superfine) sugar

Put the sugar and vanilla bean in a large
saucepan with 625 ml (21 1/2 fl oz/2 1/2 cups)
water. Stir over low heat for 8–10 minutes,
or until the sugar has dissolved. Bring to a
slow boil, then add the whole peaches and
simmer for 5 minutes, or until the peaches
are just tender and softened. Cool the
peaches in the syrup, then remove with a
slotted spoon. Peel and halve the peaches,
removing the stones.

Put the raspberries in a food processor and
process until puréed. Push the purée through
a sieve, discarding the pulp.

To make the passionfruit sauce, combine the
passionfruit pulp and sugar in a small bowl
and stir until the sugar has dissolved.

To serve, divide the raspberry purée between
4 glasses. Arrange two peach halves and a
scoop of ice cream on top. Spoon over the
passionfruit sauce and serve immediately.

To add interest to **peaches** or **nectarines** that are lacking in
flavour, cut the unpeeled fruit into wedges, then pour boiling
sugar syrup over them in a bowl — they will cook as they
cool. You can make the syrup with half red wine and half
water, and add a sprig of rosemary and a cinnamon stick,
or a few whole cloves and star anise for extra flavour.

Cointreau-glazed peaches

SERVES 6

6 freestone peaches
1–2 tablespoons soft brown sugar
4 tablespoons Cointreau
250 g (9 oz/heaped 1 cup) mascarpone
    cheese
ground nutmeg, to dust

Line a baking tray with foil and lightly grease the foil. Preheat the grill (broiler) to medium. Cut the peaches in half, remove the stones and place the peaches, cut side up, on the tray. Sprinkle the peaches with the sugar and drizzle with the Cointreau.

Place under the grill and cook for about 6 minutes, or until the peaches are soft and the tops are glazed.

Serve with dollops of mascarpone and dust lightly with nutmeg.

Amaretti-stuffed peaches

SERVES 6

6 freestone peaches
60 g (2 1/4 oz) amaretti biscuits, crushed
1 egg yolk
2 tablespoons caster (superfine) sugar,
    plus extra for sprinkling
3 tablespoons ground almonds
2 teaspoons amaretto (almond-flavoured
    liqueur)
3 tablespoons white wine
20 g (3/4 oz) unsalted butter, chopped
whipped cream, to serve

Preheat the oven to 180°C (350°F/Gas 4). Lightly grease a 30 x 25 cm (12 x 10 inch) baking dish.

Cut the peaches in half and remove the stones. Using a paring knife, scoop a little of the flesh out from each peach half to create a deeper cavity. Chop the scooped-out flesh and place it in a small bowl with the crushed biscuits, egg yolk, sugar, ground almonds and amaretto. Mix together well.

Spoon some of the stuffing mixture into each peach, then place the peaches in the baking dish, cut side up. Sprinkle with the wine and a little extra sugar. Dot with the butter and bake for 20–25 minutes, or until golden. Serve warm with whipped cream.

variation You can also use ripe apricots or nectarines for this recipe.

Peach galettes

MAKES 12

400 g (14 oz/3 1/4 cups) plain (all-purpose)
    flour
165 g (5 3/4 oz/1 1/3 cups) icing
    (confectioners') sugar, plus extra to dust
200 g (7 oz) cold unsalted butter, chopped
2 egg yolks, mixed with 2 tablespoons
    iced water

filling
600 g (1 lb 5 oz) firm ripe peaches,
    stones removed and thinly sliced
20 g (3/4 oz) unsalted butter, melted
1 tablespoon honey
1 tablespoon caster (superfine) sugar
1/4 teaspoon ground nutmeg
25 g (1 oz/1/4 cup) flaked almonds, toasted

for glazing
1 egg yolk
1 tablespoon milk
80 g (2 3/4 oz/1/4 cup) apricot jam

Sift the flour, icing sugar and a pinch of salt
into a large bowl. Using your fingertips, lightly
rub in the butter until the mixture resembles
coarse breadcrumbs. Make a well in the
centre, then add the egg yolk and water
mixture to the well. Mix using a flat-bladed
knife until a rough dough forms. Turn out
onto a lightly floured work surface, then
gently press the dough together into a ball.
Form into a flat disc, cover with plastic wrap
and refrigerate for 30 minutes.

Lightly grease a baking tray or line it with
baking paper. Roll out the pastry on a lightly
floured work surface to 3 mm (1/8 inch) thick.
Cut out twelve 12 cm (4 1/2 inch) rounds.

To make the filling, put the peach slices,
butter, honey, sugar and nutmeg in a bowl
and gently toss together. Divide the filling
among the pastry rounds, leaving a 1 cm
(1/2 inch) border around the edge. Fold the
pastry over the edge of the filling, leaving
the centre uncovered, and pleat the pastry
edges at 1 cm (1/2 inch) intervals. Place the
galettes on the baking tray and refrigerate
for 30 minutes.

Meanwhile, preheat the oven to 200°C
(400°F/Gas 6).

To make the glaze, mix together the egg yolk
and milk, then brush over the chilled pastry.
Transfer the tray to the oven and bake for
30 minutes, or until golden.

Meanwhile, put the jam and 1 tablespoon
water in a small saucepan and stir over low
heat until smooth.

Remove the galettes from the oven and
brush the jam mixture over the hot galettes.
Sprinkle with the almonds, then transfer to
a wire rack to cool slightly. Serve warm or at
room temperature, dusted with icing sugar.

plum

While a juicy sun-ripened plum requires little embellishment, this versatile fruit appears in all manner of sweet and savoury dishes from around the world, from the classic Chinese pork in plum sauce, to Germany's repertoire of plum cakes and tarts, and the French eau de vie, a clear brandy made from fermented plum juice. Plums team well with sweet spices such as cardamom, cloves, ginger and star anise and, surprisingly, they also work well with herbs such as mint, thyme and rosemary.

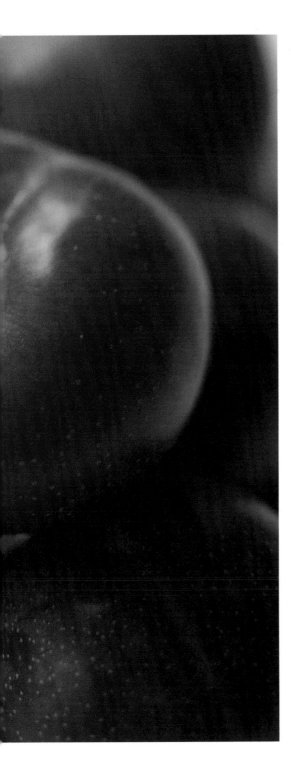

Varieties

From damsons to mirabelles, satsuma to gages, from green and yellow plums to those that are red or blue-black, there is a startling selection of plum varieties.

Broadly speaking, however, plums fall into two main groups: European plums, which are mostly used for preserving and drying (making prunes); and Japanese plums, which are actually from China. These can be either eaten fresh or used in cooking. Japanese plums are round or heart-shaped and include all the blood plum varieties.

Buying and storing

- Plums are in season from summer through to early autumn.

- Some plums may be covered with a whitish bloom; this indicates they are very fresh. Look for fruit that yield slightly when pressed.

- Choose larger, sweeter plum varieties for eating fresh or for use in desserts and baking — smaller, tart varieties are best for savoury recipes or for preserving in sugar syrup.

- Store ripe plums in the fridge for up to 2 days, and wash them just before eating.

Preparation

The skins of all varieties of plums can be sour, but will easily slip off after blanching. To skin a plum, make a small cross-shaped incision at the base with a sharp knife, then put them briefly into a bowl of boiling water. Drain and cool in a bowl of iced water, then remove and gently pull off the skin. Skinning plums may not be necessary: for jams and purées, for example, the skins can simply be sieved out.

To remove the stones, most varieties need the flesh to be cut away, although some have stones that are easily lifted out once the fruit is halved.

Plum cobbler

SERVES 6–8

750 g (1 lb 10 oz) plums (about 10 plums)
115 g (4 oz/$\frac{1}{2}$ cup) caster (superfine) sugar
125 g (4$\frac{1}{2}$ oz/1 cup) self-raising flour
60 g (2$\frac{1}{4}$ oz/$\frac{1}{2}$ cup) plain (all-purpose)
    flour
125 g (4$\frac{1}{2}$ oz) unsalted butter, chopped
1 egg
125 ml (4 fl oz/$\frac{1}{2}$ cup) milk
icing (confectioners') sugar, to dust

Preheat the oven to 180°C (350°F/Gas 4).
Lightly grease a 2 litre (70 fl oz/8 cup)
baking dish. Cut the plums into quarters,
discarding the stones.

Put the plums in a saucepan with half of the
sugar and 1 tablespoon water. Stir over low
heat for 5 minutes, or until the sugar has
dissolved and the plums have softened
slightly. Spread the plums into the dish.

Sift the flours into a bowl, add the remaining
sugar and stir to combine. Rub in the butter,
using your fingertips, until the mixture
resembles fine breadcrumbs. In a separate
bowl, combine the egg and milk and whisk
until smooth. Stir into the flour mixture until
a soft dough forms.

Drop large spoonfuls of the dough on top
of the plums, until the plums are covered
or all the mixture has been used. Bake for
30–40 minutes, or until the top is golden
and cooked through. Dust with icing sugar
before serving.

Pork noisettes with prunes

SERVES 4

16 prunes, pitted
1 tablespoon olive oil
60 g (2$\frac{1}{4}$ oz) butter
8 pork noisettes (medallions), trimmed
1 onion, finely chopped
125 ml (4 fl oz/$\frac{1}{2}$ cup) white wine
310 ml (10$\frac{3}{4}$ fl oz/1$\frac{1}{4}$ cups) chicken stock
1 bay leaf
2 thyme sprigs
250 ml (9 fl oz/1 cup) thick (double/heavy)
    cream

Put the prunes in a small saucepan, cover
with cold water and bring to the boil, then
simmer for 5 minutes. Drain and set aside.

Heat the olive oil in a large heavy-based
frying pan and add half the butter. When the
butter starts foaming, add the pork in batches
and cook over medium–high heat for about
5 minutes, or until cooked but slightly pink in
the middle, turning once. Remove to a warm
plate and cover with foil to keep warm.

Pour off any excess fat from the pan. Melt the
remaining butter in the pan, add the onion
and sauté over low heat for 5 minutes, until
softened. Add the wine, bring to the boil and
simmer for 2 minutes, then add the stock,
bay leaf and thyme and bring to the boil.
Reduce the heat and simmer for 10 minutes,
or until the mixture has reduced by half.

Strain the stock mixture into a bowl. Rinse
the frying pan and place over low heat. Add
the stock, cream and prunes and simmer for
8 minutes, or until the sauce thickens slightly.
Return the pork to the pan, simmer until
heated through and serve.

In dried form, plums are known as **prunes**. Aside from their reputation as a high-fibre fruit, they are very versatile and can be used in savoury rice pilafs, Christmas turkey stuffings or paired with almonds or hazelnuts in a tart. For a simple after-dinner treat, plump up prunes by soaking them in brandy, drain and dry with paper towels, then dip into melted chocolate.

Plum and caraway biscuits

MAKES 24

80 g (2¾ oz) unsalted butter, softened
60 g (2¼ oz/¼ cup) cream cheese, softened, chopped
115 g (4 oz/½ cup) caster (superfine) sugar
1 teaspoon natural vanilla extract
2 egg yolks
1½ teaspoons caraway seeds
150 g (5½ oz/1¼ cups) plain (all-purpose) flour
plum jam
icing (confectioners') sugar, to dust

Cream the butter, cream cheese and sugar in a bowl using electric beaters until pale and fluffy. Add the vanilla and 1 egg yolk and beat to combine well. Add the caraway seeds and flour and stir until a dough forms.

Turn the dough out onto a lightly floured work surface, form into a flat rectangle, then cover with plastic wrap and refrigerate for 2 hours, or until firm.

Preheat the oven to 180°C (350°F/Gas 4). Lightly grease two baking trays. Combine the remaining egg yolk with 2 teaspoons water and stir to combine well.

Cut the dough in half, then roll out each half on a lightly floured work surface to form an 18 x 24 cm (7 x 9½ inch) rectangle. Using a lightly floured sharp knife, cut the dough into 6 cm (2½ inch) squares.

Place a scant teaspoon of jam diagonally across the centre of each square, then brush all four corners of each square with the egg mixture. Take one corner of the square and fold it into the centre. Then take the opposite corner and fold it into the centre, overlapping the first corner slightly, to partially cover the jam and form a neat oblong shape with pointed ends.

Brush the tops of the biscuits with the egg yolk mixture, then place the biscuits, glazed side up, on the baking trays. Transfer to the oven and bake for 10–12 minutes, or until light golden, swapping the position of the trays halfway through cooking. Cool on the trays for 5 minutes, then transfer to a wire rack to cool completely. Dust with icing sugar before serving.

The biscuits will keep, stored in an airtight container, for up to 1 week.

tropical fruit

banana

Although it looks like a type of palm tree, the banana tree is actually a giant herb. Bananas grow in bunches called hands (the Arabic *banan* means 'finger'), and each hand has about 15 fingers, or fruit. Bananas are one of the few fruit that are harvested when green, as they ripen best after picking. In some countries, the stems, leaves and flowers are all used in cooking.

Varieties

Cavendish The most commonly eaten banana, these are pale-fleshed and sweet.

Red bananas These have reddish brown skin and red-tinged firm flesh that is slightly sweeter than the cavendish.

Lady's finger Also known as a sugar banana, these are a particularly sweet, flavoursome and fragrant banana often used in Asian cooking.

Plantains These starchy bananas have tough flesh that turns from green to black as they ripen. They can only be used for cooking but can be cooked whether ripe or unripe.

Buying and storing

- Bananas are available year-round but their best season is from mid-spring through to mid-autumn.

- Bananas are harvested when green and continue to ripen until their starches have all converted to sugars. It is possible to buy quite green bananas, as these will quickly ripen at room temperature.

- Bananas are at their most flavoursome when the skin is lightly flecked with black spots.

- Store bananas away from other ripe fruits, as they produce ethylene, which will cause other fruit near them to ripen prematurely. Refrigerating bananas will turn their skin black but this won't actually affect the taste.

- Very ripe bananas can be frozen for use in baking. First peel the banana, then store the flesh in an airtight plastic bag in the freezer.

Preparation

To prevent discolouration of the flesh, cut bananas just before you need them, or brush with a little lemon juice to help prevent this.

Banana fritters in coconut batter

SERVES 6

100 g (3½ oz/½ cup) glutinous rice flour (see note)
100 g (3½ oz/1 cup) freshly grated coconut, or 60 g (2¼ oz/⅔ cup) desiccated coconut
3 tablespoons sugar
1 tablespoon sesame seeds
3 tablespoons coconut milk
oil, for deep-frying
3 firm ripe bananas
ice cream, to serve

Put the rice flour, coconut, sugar, sesame seeds, coconut milk and 3 tablespoons water in a bowl and whisk until a smooth batter forms, adding a little more water if the batter is too thick. The batter should have a thick, coating consistency. Cover with plastic wrap and leave to stand for 1 hour.

Fill a wok or deep heavy-based saucepan one-third full of oil and heat to 180°C (350°F), or until a cube of bread dropped into the oil browns in 15 seconds.

Peel the bananas and cut them in half lengthways, then cut in half crossways. Working in batches, dip each piece of banana into the batter, allowing the excess batter to drain off, then gently drop into the hot oil. Cook for 4–6 minutes, or until golden brown all over. Remove the fritters with a slotted spoon and drain well on paper towels. Serve hot with ice cream.

note Glutinous rice flour is available from Asian food stores and is made by finely grinding glutinous or sticky rice; do not confuse this with ordinary rice flour as the results won't be the same.

Bananas are believed to be native to Malaysia and travelled from there to India. It was in India that Alexander the Great is thought to have first tasted them, then introduced them to the Western world. Americans first tasted the banana in 1876, in Pennsylvania, as part of the celebrations for the 100th anniversary of the signing of the Declaration of Independence.

Bananas that are past their prime can be frozen and later made into a quick dessert. Use four or five frozen bananas, break them into pieces and put in a food processor. Process until the bananas are thick and creamy. Serve in ice cream cones or small bowls.

Banana bread

MAKES 1

250 g (9 oz/2 cups) plain (all-purpose) flour
2 teaspoons baking powder
1 teaspoon mixed spice
150 g (5$\frac{1}{2}$ oz) unsalted butter, softened
185 g (6$\frac{1}{2}$ oz/1 cup) soft brown sugar
2 eggs, lightly beaten
240 g (8$\frac{1}{2}$ oz/1 cup) mashed very ripe
    banana

Preheat the oven to 180°C (350°F/Gas 4). Grease and line the base and side of a 23 x 13 x 6 cm (9 x 5 x 2$\frac{1}{2}$ inch) loaf (bar) tin.

Sift together the flour, baking powder, mixed spice and $\frac{1}{4}$ teaspoon salt into a bowl.

In a separate bowl, cream the butter and sugar using electric beaters until pale and fluffy. Add the eggs gradually, beating well after each addition, and beat until smooth. Mix in the banana. Add the dry ingredients in several batches and stir until the mixture is smooth.

Pour into the prepared tin and bake on the middle shelf of the oven for 35–45 minutes, or until a skewer inserted into the centre of the bread comes out clean. Cool in the tin for 10 minutes, then turn out onto a wire rack. Serve warm or at room temperature. Banana bread will keep for up to 3 days, covered in plastic wrap in an airtight container.

Bananas foster

SERVES 4

40 g (1$\frac{1}{2}$ oz) unsalted butter
4 firm ripe bananas, sliced in half lengthways
2 tablespoons soft brown sugar
2 tablespoons rum
vanilla ice cream, to serve

Melt the butter in a large frying pan. Add the banana halves, in batches if necessary, and briefly cook over medium–high heat, gently turning them to coat in the butter.

Add the sugar and cook for 1 minute, or until the banana is caramelised.

Sprinkle with the rum, then divide the bananas among serving plates and serve with a scoop of vanilla ice cream.

kiwi fruit

Native to China and originally called Chinese gooseberries, kiwi fruit were so-named by New Zealand growers and marketers, as it was there that the fruit was first commercially grown. There are two types: a furry-skinned type with green flesh, and a recently developed cultivar with smooth, bronze skin and yellow flesh.

Buying and storing

- Although you can generally find kiwi fruit in the markets year-round, their peak season is from summer to early winter.

- Ripe kiwi fruit should give slightly when pressed. Avoid overly soft fruit or any with wrinkled skins, as these are past their prime. If you don't intend to use them immediately, buy kiwi fruit that are still quite firm and store in the fridge for 4–5 weeks — bring them out, as needed, to ripen at room temperature.

- To speed ripening, put kiwi fruit in a paper bag with a banana or an apple, as these fruits produce ethylene gas, which will accelerate fruit ripening.

Preparation

The simplest way to prepare and use kiwi fruit is to cut them in half horizontally and scoop the flesh out with a spoon, or peel it and cut into cubes or slices.

Kiwi fruit contains an enzyme that dissolves protein — hence it is used commercially as a meat tenderiser (add a slice of kiwi fruit to your next stew or casserole). This same enzyme also inhibits the setting qualities of gelatine, so kiwi fruit are not recommended in jellies or jams.

Never use raw kiwi fruit (cooking destroys the enzyme) in dairy-based recipes; it will attack milk proteins and turn them bitter.

Pavlova with kiwi fruit

SERVES 6-8

Named for the Russian ballerina Anna Pavlova, pavlova is made from a meringue base, crisp and brittle on the outside and marshmallow-soft and chewy on the inside.

4 egg whites, at room temperature
230 g (8 oz/1 cup) caster (superfine) sugar
2 teaspoons cornflour (cornstarch)
1 teaspoon white vinegar
250 ml (9 fl oz/1 cup) whipping cream
1 banana, thinly sliced
6 strawberries, sliced
2 kiwi fruit, peeled and sliced
pulp from 3 passionfruit

Preheat the oven to 160°C (315°F/Gas 2-3). Line a 32 x 28 cm (13 x 11¼ inch) baking tray with baking paper.

Put the egg whites and a pinch of salt in a large, clean, dry stainless steel or glass bowl — any hint of grease will prevent the egg whites foaming. Using electric beaters, whisk slowly until the whites start to become foamy, then increase the speed until the bubbles in the foam have become small and even-sized. Continue whisking until stiff peaks form, then add the sugar gradually, whisking constantly after each addition, until the egg white is thick and glossy and the sugar has dissolved. Don't overbeat or the mixture will be grainy.

Using a metal spoon, fold in the sifted cornflour and the vinegar. Spoon the meringue into a mound on the prepared tray. Lightly flatten the top of the meringue and smooth the sides; the finished pavlova should have a cake shape and be about 2.5 cm (1 inch) high.

Transfer to the oven and bake for 1 hour, or until the pavlova is pale cream and crisp on the outside. Remove from the oven while warm, carefully turn upside down onto a serving plate and cool to room temperature.

Lightly whip the cream until soft peaks form and spread over the pavlova. Decorate with sliced banana, strawberries and kiwi fruit and drizzle over the passionfruit pulp. Cut into wedges to serve.

note The addition of cornflour and vinegar to the egg whites gives the meringue a soft, chewy centre.

Buying and storing

- The peak season for mangoes is from mid-spring to summer and early autumn.

- You can determine if a mango is ripe, not by its colour, which can vary according to variety, but by both its smell and feel. When ripe, mangoes should yield slightly to pressure and their stem end should smell sweet and fragrant.

- Black spots on the skin can be a sign that the flesh inside is bruised or that the fruit is overripe. Avoid mangoes with loose or wrinkled skin as these are past their best.

- Unripe fruit will ripen at room temperature. Once ripe, store in the fridge and eat within 1–2 days.

mango

The mango is often referred to as 'the king of fruits' and rightly so — many will claim it to be the world's most delicious fruit. Mangoes make their appearance in summer and the best way to eat them is fresh — in fact, more mangoes are eaten fresh than any other fruit. Mangoes also make excellent ice creams, sorbets and sauces, are great in smoothies and go well with seafood or in salads. Although grown in most tropical countries, the fruit is native to India, where they play a sacred role and are considered a symbol of love.

Varieties

There are about 350 varieties of mangoes cultivated commercially. The differences between them are basically their sweetness, amount of fibre in their flesh, the flesh-to-stone ratio and their size. Some of the more popular varieties are listed below.

Green mangoes These green-skinned hard mangoes are a popular ingredient in Southeast Asian salads, curries, pickles and chutneys. To prepare them, peel off the skin with a small knife, then either coarsely grate the flesh or cut it off the stone in very thin slices and then into fine matchsticks.

Green mango has a pleasant tart, fruity flavour, which combines well with lime juice, palm sugar (jaggery), seafood, chicken, peanuts, chilli, coriander (cilantro) and Thai basil.

Kensington pride Also known as bowen, this large fruit has particularly juicy flesh, minimal fibre and a slightly tangy flavour. Its orange skin blushes to red when ripe.

R2E2 A recently developed Australian hybrid, this very large mango has thin orange skin, very sweet flesh and a high flesh-to-stone ratio.

Kent These oval-shaped fruit have very soft, sweet and fibre-free flesh. When ripe, the skin is yellow with red shoulders.

Keitt An Indian strain of mango, these large oval-shaped fruit have lush, firm flesh, minimal fibre and thick skin. These mangoes remain green even when fully ripe.

Nam doc mai This small–medium mango has a fattish slipper shape with a long, thin stone. It is used while green in salads, curries and chutneys, but is also prized for its deep, slightly acid and sweet flavours when fully ripe.

Tommy atkins This medium–large oval mango has thick skin, a mild flavour and a more fibrous flesh than most of the others.

Mangoes not only taste glorious, they are also very good for you. High in fibre and low in calories, mangoes are also rich sources of beta-carotene and minerals, as well as vitamins A, B and C. They contain an enzyme with stomach-soothing properties which aid digestion, and perhaps may be partially responsible for that undeniable feeling of contentment you get after eating a mango.

Preparation

The mango has a large central seed that clings to the flesh, and you need to cut the mango 'cheeks' away from this. To do this, hold the mango with a narrow side facing you and using a large serrated knife, cut from the top down to the base of one side, cutting as close to the stone as possible, to remove the cheek. Repeat with the other side of the mango.

The best way to eat the flesh or remove it from the skin is to cut it into a 'hedgehog'. Use a sharp knife to score deep parallel cuts in the flesh of each cheek, then score the flesh in the other direction to create a hatched pattern. Push the skin inside out so the cubes of flesh pop out, then slice them off or eat it, as is.

Mango ice cream

SERVES 6

400 g (14 oz) fresh mango flesh
145 g (5 oz/²⁄₃ cup) caster (superfine) sugar
3 tablespoons mango or apricot nectar
250 ml (9 fl oz/1 cup) whipping cream
mango slices, extra, to serve

Put the mango in a food processor and process until smooth. Transfer the mango purée to a bowl and add the sugar and nectar. Stir until the sugar has dissolved.

Beat the cream in a small bowl until stiff peaks form and then gently fold into the mango mixture. Spoon into a shallow loaf (bar) tin, cover and freeze for 1¹⁄₂ hours, or until half frozen. Quickly spoon the mixture into a food processor and process for 30 seconds, or until smooth. Return the mixture to the tin or a plastic container, then cover and freeze completely.

Remove the ice cream from the freezer about 15 minutes before serving to allow it to soften a little. Serve the ice cream in scoops with some extra fresh mango.

Mango lassi

SERVES 4

2 large mangoes
500 g (1 lb 2 oz/2 cups) Greek-style yoghurt
2 teaspoons lemon juice
3–4 tablespoons caster (superfine) sugar,
     to taste
ice cubes, to serve
diced mango, to serve

Prepare the mangoes by slicing off the cheeks with a sharp knife. Using a large spoon, scoop the flesh from the skin. Cut the flesh into chunks and put in a blender with the yoghurt, lemon juice and 3 tablespoons of the sugar.

Add 185 ml (6 fl oz/³⁄₄ cup) cold water and blend for 40–60 seconds, or until smooth. Taste for sweetness and add the extra sugar if needed.

Put some ice cubes in the bottom of four glasses. Pour the lassi over the top and serve immediately, topped with diced mango.

To make a **mango salsa**, peel 1 small mango and finely dice the flesh. Seed 1 green chilli and finely chop the flesh. Put the mango, chilli, 2 tablespoons finely diced red onion, 2 tablespoons roughly chopped coriander (cilantro) and 1 tablespoon lime juice in a bowl. Season with sea salt and black pepper. Serve as an accompaniment to barbecued chicken or pork.

Mango and passionfruit pies

MAKES 6

400 g (14 oz/3¼ cups) plain (all-purpose)
    flour
165 g (5¾ oz/1⅓ cups) icing
    (confectioners') sugar
200 g (7 oz) cold unsalted butter, chopped
2 egg yolks, mixed with 2 tablespoons iced
    water
1 egg, lightly beaten
icing (confectioners') sugar, to dust
whipped cream, to serve

filling

4 tablespoons strained passionfruit pulp
1 tablespoon custard powder
3 ripe mangoes (900 g/2 lb), peeled, sliced
    and chopped
80 g (2¾ oz/⅓ cup) caster (superfine)
    sugar

Sift the flour and icing sugar into a large bowl. Using your fingertips, rub in the butter until the mixture resembles coarse breadcrumbs. Make a well in the centre, then add the egg yolk and water mixture to the well. Mix using a flat-bladed knife until a rough dough forms. Turn out onto a lightly floured work surface, then gently press together into a ball. Form into a flat disc, cover with plastic wrap and refrigerate for 30 minutes.

Grease six 10 x 8 x 3 cm (4 x 3¼ x 1¼ inch) fluted, loose-based tart tins.

Roll out two-thirds of the chilled dough between two sheets of baking paper until 3 mm (⅛ inch) thick. Cut out six bases to fit the prepared tins. Gently press them into the tins and trim the edges. Refrigerate for 30 minutes.

Meanwhile, preheat the oven to 190°C (375°F/Gas 5).

To make the filling, put the passionfruit pulp and custard powder in a small saucepan and mix together well. Stir over medium heat for 2–3 minutes, or until the mixture has thickened. Remove from the heat, then stir in the mango and sugar.

Roll out the remaining pastry between two sheets of baking paper until 3 mm (⅛ inch) thick. Cut out six pie lids. Reroll the pastry trimmings and cut into shapes for decoration.

Divide the filling among the pastry cases and brush the edges with beaten egg. Top with the pastry lids and press the edges to seal. Trim the edges and decorate the tops with the pastry shapes. Brush with beaten egg and dust with icing sugar.

Bake for 20–25 minutes, or until the pastry is golden. Remove from the oven and leave to cool in the tins. Serve warm or at room temperature with whipped cream.

melon

A perfect melon needs little more than to be sliced and served with a teaspoon for scooping, or in wedges to be eaten out of hand. Melons are one of those fruit that are technically a vegetable, related to other vine crops such as pumpkin, gourds and cucumbers. Melons are made up of 90 per cent water so, it goes without saying, they are very low in kilojoules.

Varieties

Sweet melons fall into two broad groups: one group includes cantaloupe, rockmelon (also known as netted melon or muskmelon) and the honeydew, and it is thought these originated in Persia, Afghanistan or Armenia; and the second group includes watermelon, which is native to Africa.

Cantaloupe True cantaloupes are grown more widely in Europe (they take their name from an Italian town called Cantalupo) and the Middle East than they are in North America or Australia — often what passes for cantaloupes in these latter countries are actually rockmelons (netted melons). True cantaloupes are smaller and rounder than these and have tougher skin that is marked in clear sections, either smooth or slightly scaly. The legendary charentais, a smallish melon with a smooth grey-green rind, and the ogen melon, a green-fleshed melon with an orange-green skin, are regarded as the aristocrats of the cantaloupe.

Honeydew A smooth melon with creamy yellow skin and sweet green flesh, these are very popular in Japan where the melon's fragrance is encapsulated by Midori liqueur.

Rockmelon Because of the raised webbing on their skin, these are also called 'netted' melons, or muskmelons on account of their lovely musky smell. Rockmelons have a netted skin with lengthwise demarcations, called sutures, and dark peach-coloured flesh.

Watermelon There are over 1000 varieties of watermelon, so named because of their high water content of around 92–95 per cent. These range in skin colour from pale green and faintly striped, to dark green with stripes. Watermelons are rounded or oval in shape and a thick protective rind lies under the skin. The sweet dark pink to red flesh contains many seeds (although there are 'seedless' varieties), which can also be roasted for snacking.

Buying and storing

- Cantaloupe, watermelon and rockmelon (netted muskmelon) are in peak season in summer; and the peak season for honeydew is in autumn.

- Unlike other melons, honeydews will continue to ripen once harvested. It's a little difficult to tell when honeydews are ripe (they are very bland when underripe); some claim the skin turns yellow when ripe, while others say it should be creamy or pale green. The most reliable method of determining ripeness is to lightly press the stem end; it should be slightly soft when the fruit is mature.

- Store ripe honeydews in the fridge for up to 4 days, but bring back to room temperature before eating. Cut honeydews should be well covered with plastic wrap, as the smell of melon permeates everything near it.

- Buy rockmelons with a deep, sweet aroma and pronounced netting on the skin — the background skin colour should be beige to golden. A ripe melon should also have a paler, slightly flattened side where it rested on the ground, and the stem end should be a little damp.

- Rockmelons are fairly perishable so eat them soon after you've bought them. Store for 1–2 days at cool room temperature, or for 2 days in the fridge.

- To tell if a watermelon is ripe, inspect the pale patch where it rested on the ground — it should be yellow, not white or light green. The skin should be matt and have a waxy rather than shiny appearance and the fruit should be large for its type and feel heavy for its size. If you tap the fruit it should sound a little hollow.

- Store watermelon for 2–3 days in the fridge, covered in plastic wrap. If it is too large to fit in the fridge, store in a cool, dark place.

While **melons** are best suited to being simply cut into wedges there are, however, some timeless dishes involving melons — from the Italians came the idea of wrapping prosciutto around melon slices; from the French, melon balls doused with port; and the Greeks combined feta and watermelon in a salad, tossed with some red onions, mint and olives. Rockmelon also goes well in cold dishes with chicken, ham and roast duck and with seafood such as prawns (shrimp), lobsters and crab.

Watermelon granita

SERVES 4

250 g (9 oz/heaped 1 cup) caster
   (superfine) sugar
1.5 kg (3 lb 5 oz) watermelon
2 tablespoons chopped mint (optional)

Put the sugar in a saucepan with 250 ml
(9 oz/1 cup) water and stir over low heat
without boiling until the sugar has dissolved.
Increase the heat and bring to the boil, then
reduce the heat and simmer, without stirring,
for 5 minutes. Pour into a large bowl to cool.

Remove the rind from the watermelon, cut
the flesh into chunks and place in a food
processor. Process the watermelon until a
purée forms, then strain, discarding the seeds
and fibre. Mix the watermelon purée with the
sugar syrup and pour into a shallow metal
tray. Freeze for 1 hour, or until ice crystals
start to form around the edges.

After this time, remove from the freezer and
use a fork to scrape the frozen edges back
into the mixture. Return to the freezer. Repeat
this process at least twice more, or until the
mixture has large, even-sized ice crystals. For
refreshing extra flavour, add 2 tablespoons
chopped mint when freezing the last time.

Serve immediately or beat well with a fork
and refreeze until ready to serve. Scrape the
granita into serving dishes with a fork, or
serve in scoops in tall glasses.

Watermelon, feta and watercress salad

SERVES 4

2 tablespoons sunflower seeds
1 kg (2 lb 4 oz) seedless watermelon
180 g (6 oz/1 ¼ cups) crumbled feta cheese
100 g (3 ½ oz) watercress sprigs
2 tablespoons olive oil
1 tablespoon lemon juice
2 teaspoons chopped oregano

Heat a small frying pan over medium–high
heat. Add the sunflower seeds and, shaking
the pan continuously, dry-fry for 2 minutes,
or until lightly golden. Quickly remove the
pan from the heat and tip the seeds into a
bowl so they don't burn.

Cut the rind away from the watermelon, then
cut the flesh into thick wedges. Place in a
large serving dish along with the feta and
watercress and toss gently to combine.

In a small bowl, whisk together the olive oil,
lemon juice and oregano. Season to taste
with a little sea salt and freshly ground black
pepper (don't add too much salt as the feta
is already quite salty).

Pour the dressing over the salad and gently
toss together. Scatter with the toasted
sunflower seeds and serve.

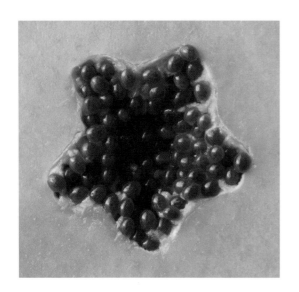

papaya

The taste of a ripe papaya is unforgettable — musky–sweet yet mildly bitter, and distinctly floral. The black seeds, which are usually discarded, are edible and have a peppery flavour. The soft flesh is best enjoyed raw, tossed through fruit salads, whipped into orange-based drinks or just spooned directly from its skin.

Buying and storing

- Papayas are sold year-round in markets but their peak season is from late spring through to early autumn.

- Papayas are often labelled in shops as 'pawpaws' — the pawpaw is actually a wild American fruit and is completely unrelated to the papaya.

- There are two main varieties available — the larger, pear-shaped yellow papaya with orange, slightly pungent-smelling flesh, and the smaller, sweeter, rose-fleshed type.

- Papayas continue to ripen once picked (leave them in a dark place at room temperature for several days to ripen) but their flavour suffers when not fully tree-ripened. Ripe papayas will yield to gentle pressure and they may have slightly spotted skin, with no traces of green.

- Store ripe papayas in the fridge and use within 2 days. Cover any cut portions with plastic wrap as they have a strong smell.

Preparation

Papayas, particularly unripe ones, contain a whitish liquid from which papain is extracted. Papain is an enzyme that breaks down protein and is used to tenderise meat. It also prevents gelatine from setting, so papaya is not a good choice for desserts such as jellies.

Chopped papaya can cause fruit in a fruit salad to soften if left for a while, so add it just before serving, and sprinkle with a little lime juice or lemon to bring out the flavour.

Like mango, hard, unripe green papaya is used in Southeast Asian cooking as a vegetable, mainly shredded in salads, and dressed with the tart, spicy, sweet flavours of lime juice, fish sauce, palm sugar (jaggery), chilli and garlic.

Papaya lime fool

SERVES 4

2 ripe papayas
1–2 tablespoons lime juice
3 tablespoons vanilla sugar (see notes)
315 ml (10¾ fl oz/1¼ cups) whipping cream

Peel the papayas, remove the seeds and mash the flesh until smooth. Do not do this in a food processor or the purée will be too thin. Add the lime juice and vanilla sugar, to taste — the amount will vary according to the sweetness of the fruit.

Whip the cream until soft peaks form, then fold through the mashed papaya. Spoon into serving glasses and chill until ready to serve.

notes You can make your own vanilla sugar by storing a vanilla bean in a jar of sugar. Keep the jar sealed for about 2 weeks before using it. Split the bean and disperse the seeds into the sugar for a stronger flavour.

As a variation, 500 g (1 lb 2 oz) stewed rhubarb can be substituted for the papaya. If using rhubarb, replace the lime juice with the same amount of orange juice.

Chicken and green papaya salad

SERVES 4

250 ml (9 fl oz/1 cup) coconut cream
200 g (7 oz) boneless, skinless chicken
    breasts, trimmed
200 g (7 oz/1 cup) jasmine rice, rinsed well
375 ml (13 fl oz/1½ cups) coconut milk
2 garlic cloves, chopped
3 red Asian shallots, chopped
3 small red chillies
1 teaspoon small dried shrimp
2 tablespoons fish sauce
8 cherry tomatoes, halved
150 g (5 oz) green papaya, grated
2 tablespoons lime juice
2 large handfuls mint, chopped
2 large handfuls coriander (cilantro), sliced

Bring the coconut cream to a boil in a small saucepan. Add the chicken and simmer over low heat for 5 minutes. Turn off the heat and cover the pan for 20 minutes. Remove the chicken from the pan and shred it.

Put the washed rice and coconut milk in a small saucepan and bring to the boil. Reduce the heat to low, cover and simmer for 20 minutes. Remove from the heat and leave the lid on until ready to serve.

Using a mortar and pestle or blender, pound or blend the garlic, shallots and chillies together. Add the shrimp and fish sauce and pound to break up the dried shrimp. Add the tomatoes and pound together to form a rough paste.

Combine the shredded chicken and chilli paste mixture in a bowl, then add the grated papaya, lime juice, mint and coriander. Serve with the hot coconut rice.

passionfruit

This fruit, with its tough, protective exterior and seedy and intensely fragrant pulpy interior, is, for many, a true symbol of the tropics. The most common variety is purple-skinned but some are yellow or orange. To enjoy passionfruit in its purest form, simply cut the fruit in half and scoop out the sweet but tart, juicy pulp.

Buying and storing

- Passionfruit are in season from late summer to early autumn.

- Purple passionfruit should be avoided if the skin is smooth, as these will be too tart. When ripe, their skins thin a little and become wrinkled.

- The lighter yellow varieties are ripe when smooth and have a little 'give'.

- Store for 1 week at cool room temperature, or in the fridge for up to 3 weeks. Both passionfruit pulp and the strained juice can be frozen.

Preparation

Although the seeds are edible, some recipes may ask for them to be strained out. To do this, push the pulp through a sieve using the back of a spoon, pressing firmly on the seeds to extract as much juice as possible.

As a rough guide, 1 passionfruit will yield about 1 tablespoon (20 g/^{3}/4 oz) of pulp.

A little passionfruit goes a long way — its concentrated, fruity flavours quickly pervade whatever it is added to. Add to drinks, icing for cakes, to shortbread dough and fruit salads. Drizzle the pulp over yoghurt, ice cream and other creamy desserts.

Passionfruit melting moments

MAKES 14

250 g (9 oz) unsalted butter, softened
40 g (1 1/2 oz/1/3 cup) icing (confectioners')
   sugar
1 teaspoon natural vanilla extract
185 g (6 1/2 oz/1 1/2 cups) self-raising flour
60 g (2 1/4 oz/1/2 cup) custard powder

passionfruit filling
60 g (2 1/4 oz) unsalted butter, softened
60 g (2 1/4 oz/1/2 cup) icing (confectioners')
   sugar
1 1/2 tablespoons strained passionfruit pulp

Preheat the oven to 180°C (350°F/Gas 4).
Line two baking trays with baking paper.

Using electric beaters, cream the butter and
icing sugar in a large bowl until light and fluffy.
Add the vanilla and beat until combined. Sift
the flour and custard powder into a bowl,
then stir into the butter mixture until a soft
dough forms.

Roll level tablespoons of the mixture into
28 balls and place on the baking trays,
spacing them well apart to allow for
spreading. Flatten the balls slightly with
a fork. Bake for 20 minutes, or until lightly
golden, then transfer to a wire rack to cool.

To make the passionfruit filling, cream the
butter and icing sugar in a small bowl using
electric beaters until light and fluffy, then stir
in the passionfruit pulp.

Use the passionfruit filling to sandwich pairs
of the cooled biscuits together. Leave to firm
before serving.

The biscuits will keep for up to 4 days, stored
in a cool place in an airtight container.

variations To make a coffee filling, dissolve
2 teaspoons instant coffee granules in
2 teaspoons water and beat it into the
creamed butter mixture instead of the
passionfruit pulp.

Melting moments can also be piped for a
decorative finish. Using a large, strong piping
(icing) bag fitted with a large star nozzle, pipe
the biscuit mixture in heaped rounds, about
3.5 cm (1 1/4 inches) wide at the base, directly
onto two large baking trays lined with baking
paper, allowing room for spreading.
Refrigerate for 30 minutes, or until firm, then
bake as directed above.

Hot passionfruit soufflé

SERVES 4

2 egg yolks
125 g (4 1/2 oz/1/2 cup) passionfruit pulp
   (from about 6 passionfruit)
2 tablespoons lemon juice
90 g (3 1/4 oz/3/4 cup) icing (confectioners')
   sugar
6 egg whites
icing (confectioners') sugar, to dust

passionfruit sauce
4 tablespoons passionfruit pulp
   (from about 4 passionfruit)
2 tablespoons caster (superfine) sugar

Preheat the oven to 210°C (415°F/Gas 6–7). Place a collar of baking paper to come about 3 cm (1 1/4 inches) above the outside of four 125 ml (4 fl oz/1/2 cup) ramekins. Tie the collars securely with string. Lightly grease the ramekins (including the paper) and sprinkle the inside of the dishes with a little caster sugar, shaking out any excess.

Combine the egg yolks, passionfruit pulp, lemon juice and half the icing sugar in a large bowl. Whisk until well combined.

Using electric beaters, whisk the egg whites in a clean, dry bowl until soft peaks form. Gradually add the remaining icing sugar, beating well after each addition.

Using a large metal spoon, fold the egg white mixture in batches into the passionfruit mixture. Divide the mixture among the four ramekins. Using a flat-bladed knife, cut through the mixture in a circular motion, about 2 cm (3/4 inch) in from the edge.

Put the ramekins on a large baking tray and transfer to the oven. Bake the soufflés for 20–25 minutes, or until well risen and cooked through.

While the soufflés are cooking, make the passionfruit sauce. Combine the passionfruit pulp and sugar in a small bowl and stir until the sugar has dissolved. Set aside.

Remove the collars from the ramekins and serve the soufflés immediately, drizzled with the passionfruit sauce and dusted with sifted icing sugar.

Originally from South America, the **passionfruit** was named by Spanish missionaries who saw in parts of its flower various references to Christ's passion — the five wounds in the anthers, the three nails in the stigmas and the crown of thorns in the filaments.

Passionfruit tart

SERVES 8

135 g (4¾ oz) plain (all-purpose) flour
3 tablespoons icing (confectioners') sugar
3 tablespoons custard powder
45 g (1½ oz) unsalted butter, cut into cubes
4 tablespoons evaporated milk

filling
125 g (4 oz/½ cup) ricotta cheese
   (see note)
1 teaspoon natural vanilla extract
30 g (1 oz/¼ cup) icing (confectioners')
   sugar
2 eggs, lightly beaten
4 tablespoons passionfruit pulp
   (about 4 passionfruit)
185 ml (6 fl oz/¾ cup) evaporated milk
icing (confectioners') sugar, to dust

Preheat the oven to 200°C (400°F/Gas 6). Lightly grease a 23 cm (8½ inch) loose-based tart tin.

Sift the flour, icing sugar and custard powder into a bowl and rub in the butter until crumbs form. Add enough evaporated milk to form a soft dough. Turn out on a lightly floured surface, bring the dough together, then gather into a ball, cover in plastic wrap and refrigerate for 15 minutes.

Roll the dough out on a lightly floured surface, large enough to fit the tin. Trim the excess pastry using a sharp knife, then refrigerate for 15 minutes. Line the pastry shell with baking paper and half-fill with baking beads or rice. Bake for 10 minutes, then remove the beads and paper and bake for another 5–8 minutes, or until golden. Allow to cool.

Reduce the oven to 160°C (315°F/Gas 2–3). To make the filling, beat the ricotta with the vanilla and icing sugar until smooth. Add the eggs, passionfruit pulp and evaporated milk, then beat well. Put the tin with the pastry case on a baking tray and pour in the filling. Bake for 40 minutes, or until set. Leave to cool in the tin before transferring to a serving plate. Dust with icing sugar to serve.

note Buy fresh ricotta cheese from the delicatessen or cheese shop, as it has a better texture and flavour than the ricotta sold in tubs. Drain well before use.

pineapple

Luscious, juicy pineapple needs little to improve upon its raw perfection and is best enjoyed in sweet slices, as well as in fruit salads or cakes. But it's also sublime in savoury dishes such as curries, as its gentle acidity cuts the richness of meats such as pork and duck. Generally, pineapples aren't sold by variety: they are usually classed as 'rough-leafed' or 'smooth-leafed'. The former are particularly aromatic and have sweet, dark golden flesh, while the latter are large, very juicy when ripe, but not as sweet as 'roughies'.

Buying and storing

- The peak season for pineapples is from mid-winter to summer.

- Pineapples don't continue to ripen after picking and are often harvested a little early. To choose a good pineapple, let your nose be your guide — the fruit should smell sweet. Another test for ripeness is to pull out a leaf from the crown — if it comes away easily, it is ripe.

- The colour of the skin doesn't necessarily indicate the ripeness of the fruit. Depending on the variety, the skin can be golden, reddish yellow or even green-tinged.

- Store ripe pineapples at room temperature for no longer than 1–2 days, or in the fridge for up to 4 days, in a plastic bag and with the leaves still attached.

Preparation

To trim and peel a pineapple, first cut off the leafy top, then cut off the base. Stand the fruit upright on the cut base and run your knife down the side, cutting off the thick skin in strips.

To remove the 'eyes', use a small knife to cut v-shaped grooves that follow the pattern of the eyes around the fruit. Slice the pineapple in half lengthways, and cut out the tough core, then cut into slices or dice.

Pineapple contains bromelin, an enzyme that breaks down protein (similar to the papain in papaya). Don't use raw pineapple in jellies, as the bromelin will prevent the gelatine setting, and don't combine it with cream or yoghurt (unless stirred in just before serving) as it will cause them to separate. Heat destroys the enzyme so you can make jellies and uncooked cheesecakes with pineapple that has first been cooked (or tinned).

Coriander pork with fresh pineapple

SERVES 4

400 g (14 oz) pork loin or fillet, trimmed
1/4 pineapple
1 tablespoon vegetable oil
4 garlic cloves, chopped
4 spring onions (scallions), chopped
1 tablespoon fish sauce
1 tablespoon lime juice
1 large handful coriander (cilantro)
1 large handful mint, chopped
steamed rice, to serve

Place the pork in the freezer for 15 minutes, or until it is just firm, then slice thinly. Cut the skin off the pineapple, then cut the flesh into bite-sized pieces.

Heat the oil in a wok or heavy-based frying pan. Add the garlic and spring onions and cook over medium–high heat for 1 minute. Remove from the wok.

Heat the wok until very hot, then add the pork in batches and stir-fry for 2–3 minutes, or until just cooked. Return the garlic, spring onions and all the pork to the wok and add the pineapple, fish sauce and lime juice. Toss together, then cook for 1 minute, or until the pineapple is heated through.

Toss the coriander and mint through and serve immediately, with steamed rice.

Sweet drunken pineapple

SERVES 6

1 large pineapple
oil, for brushing
40 g (1 1/2 oz/1/4 cup) grated palm sugar (jaggery) or soft brown sugar
2 1/2 tablespoons rum
2 tablespoons lime juice
3 tablespoons small mint leaves
thick (double/heavy) cream, to serve

Preheat a barbecue grill or chargrill pan to medium. Trim the ends from the pineapple, cut off the skin and then cut into quarters lengthways. Brush the grill with oil, then cook the pineapple quarters for about 10 minutes, turning to brown all the cut sides.

Take the pineapple off the heat and cut each quarter into 1.5 cm (5/8 inch) thick slices. Overlap the slices on a large serving plate.

Combine the sugar, rum and lime juice in a small bowl, mixing well to dissolve the sugar. Pour the mixture evenly over the warm pineapple slices, then cover with plastic wrap and refrigerate for several hours. Serve at room temperature, sprinkled with the mint leaves and a dollop of cream.

Index

Published in 2009 by Murdoch Books Pty Limited

Murdoch Books Australia
Pier 8/9
23 Hickson Road
Millers Point NSW 2000
Phone: +61 (0) 2 8220 2000
Fax: +61 (0) 2 8220 2558
www.murdochbooks.com.au

Murdoch Books UK Limited
Erico House
6th Floor, 93–99 Upper Richmond Road
Putney, London SW15 2TG
Phone: +44 (0) 20 8785 5995
Fax: +44 (0) 20 8785 5985
www.murdochbooks.co.uk

Chief Executive: Juliet Rogers
Publishing Director: Kay Scarlett

Commissioning editor: Lynn Lewis
Senior designer: Heather Menzies
Design concept and design: Jacqueline Richards
Editor: Kim Rowney
Additional text: Leanne Kitchen
Production: Elizabeth Malcolm
Photographers: Steve Brown, Natasha Milne, George Seper
Cover photography: Stuart Scott
Stylists: Marie-Hélène Clauzon, Sarah O'Brien
Food preparation: Joanne Glynn
Recipes: Murdoch Books test kitchen

Seasonal availabilities are given only as a guide; regional differences may apply.

National Library of Australia Cataloguing-in-Publication entry
Title: Cooking from the market – fruit
ISBN: 9781741965452 (pbk.)
Notes: Includes index.
Subjects: Cookery (Fruit)
  Fruit--Handling.
  Fruit--History.
Other Authors/Contributors: Lewis, Lynn.
Dewey Number: 641.64
A catalogue record for this book is available from the British Library.

PRINTED IN CHINA